For my husband Michael, my *Thlem Goyn*,
whose love enabled this book to be written.

CONTENTS

Wong/Jiang Family Tree

Ah Ngange (Father's Mother)

Wong Gay Sieng (Adoptive Father) AKA Ah Yea, Ah Gay Sieng

(M)

Lee Tew May (Adoptive Mother) AKA Ah Ma, Ah Tew May, Ah Ngange

ADOPTED

Jiang Poy Lim (Father, Nov 7, 1877–May 26, 1960) AKA Ah Yea, Ah Poy Lim

(M)

Loo Shee (Mother, Oct 3, 1880–July 22, 1958) AKA Ah Shee, Ah Hoo

Liang Family (Birth parents)

Wong Guey Dang (Oct 10, 1902– Dec 23, 1983) AKA Ah Dang, Ah Libp Thlange

(M)

Jiang Tew Thloo (4th daughter, Jan 11, 1911–Dec 12, 2002) AKA Ah Thloo, Jang Tue Sue Wong

Jiang Tew Fuy (1st daughter, died young)

Guan Haw One (1934–2009) AKA Ah One

(M)

Wong Lai Quen (1st daughter, 1935–) AKA Ah Lai

Jiang Gim Yoke (1st son) AKA Ah Goo M–no children

Guan Bing Fuy (1st daughter) AKA Ah Fuy M–1 daughter

Guan Bing Doon (Son) AKA Ah Doon M–2 daughters

Guan Samoy (2nd daughter) AKA Ah Samoy, Ah Thlam Moy M–no children

Jiang Tew May (2nd daughter) AKA Ah Ngay Day M–1 son, 4 daughters

Jiang Tew Ngoke (3rd daughter) AKA Ah Thlam Day M–1 son

Huo Li Sheung (1947–) AKA Ah Sheung

(M)

Wong Yuet Wei (Son, 1948–2001) AKA Ah Wei, Robert

Michael Henry Cockerell (1950–) AKA Ah Mikoo

(M)

Wong May Quen (2nd daughter, 1955–) AKA Ah May

Jiang Ngien Choo (2nd son) AKA Ah Choo M–3 sons, 1 daughter

Introduction

My parents' unique voices are an integral part of me. It was almost impossible to get Daddy to talk about his childhood or about his early life in Canada, but occasionally, if I was very insistent, he would dole out tidbits. Unlike the search for fonder memories, he never tried hard to recapture the details of the difficult parts of his life. "Too long ago, now," he would say dismissively in his pidgin English. "I can lememba no more."

I have supplemented my memories of his snippets by recording conversations over the years with my mother, family, and friends, and adding to that information by searching through long-forgotten documents, examining old photographs, reading history books, and collecting government records. These artifacts are like small, uneven patches woven together in a quilt, which I hope has created an understandable pattern of the life my father lived.

Like the music of favourite songs, I can still clearly hear my mother's voice telling me the stories of their separate lives. We lived together for thirty-nine years, with a brief interlude, but it was only during the last sixteen years, when she came to live with my husband and me, that I paid close attention and understood the significance of her life's history. I didn't start writing until after Mommy had passed away, and over the eight years it has taken to complete it, she spoke to me in my dreams, urging and encouraging.

Mommy only ever spoke Chinese to me. At first, Daddy spoke only Chinese too, but I have stronger memories of his English. I hope to bring them closer to the reader by including Chinese words and sentences in their native Hoyping dialect and my father's use of pidgin English. I created the phonetic spelling of the Hoyping words and because they are based on my own elementary fluency, I take full blame for any inaccuracies. The Glossary with English and Pinyin will help the reader with translations. The names of places, other than the villages my parents knew (in Hoyping), are written in Pinyin (e.g., Beijing rather than Peking).

I have provided only a sliver of the political, social, and cultural influences that touched my parents' lives, both in China and in Canada. They certainly lived in interesting times—any omissions and errors in recording that history are mine alone.

Guey Dang Wong and Tue Sue Wong, *circa* 1970.
FEELOW STUDIO, MONTREAL

Called Back

I once called my mother back from the brink of death. I was too late for my father—before he died, he didn't even recognize me. It wasn't until after both of them had died that I understood why my mother had so much to forgive and learned how my father had reinvented himself over his lifetime.

At first opium had been actually smoked like tobacco ... the smoke was about 0.2 percent morphine, quite mild. But in the late eighteenth century smokers began to put a little globule or bolus of pure opium extract in a pipe over a flame and inhale the heated water-and-opium vapor, which was about 9 or 10 percent morphine, a powerful narcotic ... The Anglo-American shippers brought opium legally by their own laws to the China Coast, whence Chinese smugglers took it illegally by Chinese law into the country.

—John King Fairbank, *The Great Chinese Revolution, 1800–1985*

ONE

Father Reclaimed

AH DANG: CHINA, 1908–1921

"Ah Doy, Boy, you have been chosen," his father said, roughly pushing the six-year-old out the door of the hovel.

The young boy struggled to understand what he had heard. His father had hardly ever spoken directly to him before. Why had he been singled out? What did his father mean by "chosen," and for what? While he wanted to know the answers, it was not his place to ask. He didn't say anything, only hung his head and listened. The rest of the family—his mother, his older brothers and sisters—were listening too. The hut they all lived in was too small to keep secrets. The wattle walls had so many chunks broken out of them that sounds were heard as if through a honeycomb.

"You are lucky," his father said. "Your new family will take good care of you, and you will have rice to eat every day."

At that, the child looked up briefly at his father. Daily meals were an unheard-of luxury. Just thinking about the possibility made his distended but empty stomach grumble loudly and his mouth water. What did his father mean about a new family? Seeking clarification, he stole another glance upward, but the man was no longer paying him any attention. Instead, he was staring at a small red envelope clutched tightly in his trembling hands and bowing obsequiously to a well-dressed stranger.

He had been sold. He had known other children in their neighbourhood who had suddenly left home, never to be seen again, and his siblings told him they had been sold. Suddenly understanding his fate, the boy felt discarded. His mouth immediately turned dry when just a second ago he had been almost drooling. His heart started to pound, making it hard to breathe, his ears rang, and his face and scalp were hot and had turned red. He felt ashamed, not knowing what he had unwittingly done to deserve this punishment, and he was suddenly afraid—of what, he did not know. He had no name for the fear; he just felt his skin go clammy and cold.

He didn't hear his new father being introduced to him. Neither was he aware of his own father's last instructions to obey and follow in the man's footsteps. Blindly responding to a gentle push on his bony back by the stranger's hand, he started to walk, dragging his bare feet forward. He left the village forever. He didn't notice until the end of the trip that he had ridden in a rickshaw for the first time in his short life. When he became aware of his new surroundings, he found that everything had changed.

Until then, the boy had been the youngest child of the Liang family, with many brothers and sisters. His parents, landless peasant farmers, had long depended more on their children's wiles than their own labours to bring food into the house. Floods and pestilence had ravaged the country, and the tiny plot of land the family leased to raise food had not been spared. The soil was as barren and dry as a piece of chewed-up sugar cane. The children lived through cunning—begging, scrounging, and even stealing anything edible. They scraped the hillocks and fields clean of twigs and grasses for *chai*, kindling, and sold the small bundles on market days for rare copper coins, which they turned over to their father. What little money their father could hoard, he wasted mostly on gambling, praying to the gods for luck. It seemed the gods were too busy dispensing luck elsewhere.

Their father had another escape; he always kept enough coins for a few plugs of opium. Although the Imperial government had banned the use and sale of opium in 1796, China had been forced to allow the British to trade in the drug after the country was defeated in the Opium Wars of 1842 and 1860. In 1908, the year the youngest Liang boy was sold, it was still readily available. For many peasants, opium was the only relief they had from the torturously slow deaths they knew as their lives.

For the boy's father, smoking the sweet pipe into a dream-filled sleep was a vain attempt to forget his bitter failures. There were too many mouths to feed and not enough of anything, and the pressures of hunger, poverty, and hopelessness were too much to bear unaided. His solution was to offer his youngest son for sale to a man of means.

Thus, the boy became the only son of two strangers of the Wong clan. The relatively prosperous couple had sought a boy to bring home and raise as their own, a replacement for their own dead infant son.

In Confucian China, a male child carried the hopes and dreams of a family. More importantly, a son projected the historical significance of the family into the future and ensured that ancestors would be remembered and cared for. Family shrines in the home and at gravesites needed regular tending. Daily offerings were made at the shrine, and in most households, these would be paper offerings, respectful sentiments written on red streamers. Incense would be lit, lifting the family's prayers on fragrant spirals to heaven. Richer families added presents of small cups filled with wine, bowls of fruit, and platters of cooked meats.

Each spring, during the national festival called Qing Ming, meaning "Clear and Bright," families visited their ancestral gravesites, identified by colourful markers, and the men of the family would sweep and tidy the small mounds where their ancestors' bones were buried. They led the family in paying their respects with *kowtows*, low bows, arranged food offerings, and reminisced about the deceased. All those present shared the picnic fare with the dead.

Families without children but with financial means could buy or "adopt" a son to carry on the family line and traditions. Girls were also adopted. In less wealthy families, this was an inexpensive way to groom a future daughter-in-law, but most often, the girls became, at best, household servants.

Until the day the boy was sold, he had answered to the listless, absent-minded call of Ah Doy, Boy. All the boys in his family were addressed similarly, just as all the girls were called Ah Nui, Girl. It was as if his parents had never bothered to name their children or, from hopeless weariness, could no longer recall their identities. At his new home, he was told his ancestral or family name would be Wong and his given names Guey Dang, which he later learned meant "Great Praise." His adoptive parents called him Ah Dang.

Before the move, the boy had lived in the village of Nam Hange in the county of Yin Pange, in the southern province of Guangdong. His home had been built of woven bamboo stalks, plugged irregularly with daubs of dried cow dung. A lotus leaf would have provided better shelter from the elements, but it had been the place where he had slept among his siblings, crammed together like pups in a litter.

Ah Dang had no recollection of the trip to his new house, still in Guangdong Province, but in a village seemingly far away from his former home. His new village was called Wong Nai Woo, in the county of Hoyping. The couple who adopted him owned a large house of yellow clay with thick walls. It was so well built that, though it was set on fire by roving bandits not long after Ah Dang had arrived, only the wooden roof beams burned and the house could be rebuilt. However, his mother thought their house had already been targeted, and while the family had been physically unharmed, it would surely tempt the gods to remain in the village. Feeling vulnerable, they abandoned the house and left Wong Nai Woo.

Auspiciously, they were invited to build a house in a newly established hamlet called Longe Gonge Lay by another Wong family, consisting of several brothers and their families. One of the elders, Ah Ngay Gonge, Second Elder Uncle, knew Ah Dang's father. This elder would later play a crucial role in Ah Dang's own life. In Longe Gonge Lay, Ah Dang's family lived for years in a small, one-room house hastily built by his father.

The boy had always known hunger; a dizzying, gut-cramping, growling hunger, and he was emaciated. The only *thlonge*, any accompaniment for rice, he had ever known was a watery, salty sauce to help relieve the boring, bland taste of coarse brown rice.

Upon his arrival at his new home, the woman who told him to call her Ah Ma, Mother, gave him a whole bowl of *faan*, cooked rice, for himself. Even more incredibly, it was topped with small, tender pieces of meat. He had seen and smelled braised meats for sale at the market, and had once managed to taste a scrap, carelessly discarded by the meat seller. Now, the tantalizing aroma made him salivate. He had never had so much to eat before, and did not stop shovelling the meal down his throat until he saw the bottom of the bowl. Almost immediately afterwards, he was sick with cramps, vomiting, and diarrhea. His new mother cleaned him up. Later, she gave him smaller portions, gradually allowing him to build up tolerance and stamina, and she cooked special soups to nourish and heal his damaged young body.

"Ah Doy," Ah Ma said, her voice giving an affectionate tone to the term, "slowly, slowly, eat." Being resilient, he soon ate as much as the grown-ups and he started to fill out and grow.

His adoptive mother was named Tew May and she had been born of the Lee family. She was a small, wiry woman. Her hands, unusually large for her size, had thick, strong, blunt fingers, used to doing manual labour in and outside of the house. She worked tirelessly in the fields. She had a long, narrow face, with dark, deep-set, hard-looking eyes, and creases, like crevices on the face of a stone statue, bracketed her mouth. Together, her features looked as though they had been dug in and dragged down by a hard and unfulfilling life.

Ah Tew May had longed for a child, but her husband worked and lived in Canada for extended periods, and his homecomings were rare and unpredictable in time and duration. After a number of miscarriages, she had finally borne a son; his recent death had added a crushing blow. Ah Dang was to be the dead child's replacement and would be known as "Second Son."

At his former home, the boy had worn faded and ill-patched hand-me-downs from his brothers. His feet had never known shoes. The kind-faced man who had brought him to this place, who told the boy to call him Ah Yea, Father, gave him a pair of short pants, a shirt, and a pair of straw sandals, none of which had ever been worn by anyone else. The stiff cotton of the shirt scratched his neck and armpits; the sandals chafed his flat feet and gave him blisters.

"Don't worry," Ah Yea said. "The sandals will eventually break in with wearing."

It turned out they never did, as Ah Dang hardly ever wore them before his feet grew out of them. He preferred to walk in his bare feet, which were leathery and calloused; he was never comfortable in shoes of any kind.

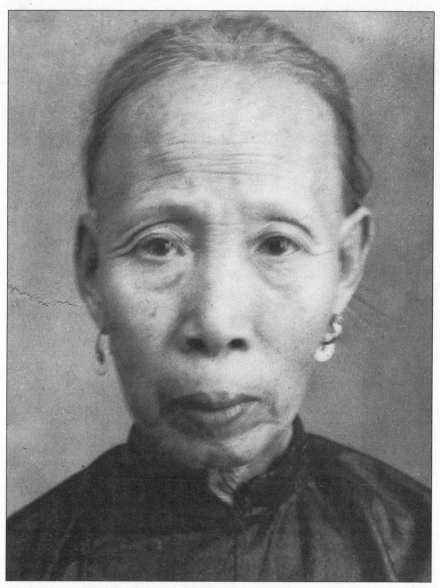

Wong Tew May, Ah Dang's adoptive mother, *circa* 1920s.
UNKNOWN PHOTOGRAPHER, CHINA

He never got used to his new mother either. Their relationship was complicated and Ah Dang had a mind of his own from the start. Later, it would be said of him, "Since childhood, he has had no training," meaning either that no one had taught him or he was too stubborn to listen and learn.

It took some time for him to forget his other family, but eventually even random thoughts of playing with his siblings no longer entered his mind. He continued to be lonely, but not for them. When Ah Dang was in his teens, Ah Tew May brought home a little girl, who was called Ah Moydoy. He never thought of her as his sister, only as his adoptive mother's daughter.

Ah Dang reasoned that if his birth family could abandon him, he must become self-sufficient and contained. Yearning for the familiar company of his brothers and sisters had not filled the gap in his life or erased the pain in his heart. He apparently no longer had to prove his worth by being obedient or contributing to the new family. If these people kept feeding and clothing him, despite what he did or said, it was their choice. If they sold him to someone else, it was their choice. If they brought in other children, it was also their choice. He could not let himself feel love, only to risk being discarded again. So he tested them by disobeying the woman who insisted he call her Ah Ma and spurning any overt signs of affection from her.

Ah Tew May reacted to his wilfulness quickly and with raw anger. She had a fiery disposition and a sharp tongue; she became a stern disciplinarian. If kind words and caring did not make Ah Dang an obedient son, she would beat him into submitting to her will. She immediately transferred her tender care and affection to Ah Moydoy.

One incident remained clearly etched in Ah Dang's mind, and whenever he told his children, in his pidgin English, he would laugh and shake his head. His mother was chasing him, wielding her sharp cleaver above her head in one large hand and shouting angrily at him. "She so mat at me, she chase me all deway to pon, she want cut off my het! She stap only when I jum in wada!"

Ah Dang had a very different relationship with his father, Wong Gay Sieng. A handsome man, he had a calm face, with a high, smooth forehead, intelligent eyes, and a full, sensuous mouth. Although unsmiling in his photographs, he managed to convey a sense of kindness and openness, and Ah Dang responded to his quiet demeanour and undemanding ways.

Ah Gay Sieng was a Gim San law, a Gold Mountain Man, a man who had gone to America. He spent much of his life in Canada, which was also called Gim San. Although the Canadian Gold Rush was long over when he arrived, the name stuck, and dreams of walking on streets paved with gold bricks lingered in the minds of hopeful immigrants. It is unclear when Ah Gay Sieng first went to Canada or how many times he was able to return to China to visit his wife, but he had initially been sponsored by his brother-in-law. No one now knows about the work he did while he was in the new country.

Most Chinese immigrants at that time were peasant farmers or unskilled labourers, working at physically demanding jobs. Asking only the lowest wages, they did laundry, washed dishes, cooked at logging camps, and cleaned and canned fish. Some added to their income by growing vegetables and selling their produce door to door.

A very few were businessmen, diplomats, or students. Ah Gay Sieng seems to have had business acumen, as his photographs invariably show him in Western business garb—a suit, tie, and leather brogues—rather than labourers' clothing. A clue to the authenticity of the clothes is that they fit him, making it unlikely he had borrowed or rented them just for posing in pictures.

He also had kinship ties that provided access to financial resources. In China, he could afford to abandon the family house that had been burned by bandits to start over with a large lot in a new hamlet. To ensure family continuity, he was able to buy a son. He did not go into debt to pay the Canadian head tax required of Chinese immigrants.

Ah Dang was respectful with Ah Gay Sieng. Here was a man on whom he could rely: someone who was self-sufficient and successful, who didn't need opium to forget his failures, who made his own luck. He seemed to epitomize his name, Gay Sieng, which meant "Remembering Constancy."

While Ah Gay Sieng spent much of Ah Dang's growing-up years away, working in Canada, the boy did not feel deserted. His father faithfully supported the family, sending remittance cheques back regularly, although many other Gim San law abandoned their families after they left China. He insisted the boy attend school. He wrote letters to his son, telling him stories of the wonders of the distant land as an incentive for him to continue his studies and to prepare him for a life away from the hamlet.

In 1921, when Ah Dang was eighteen years old, he too left for Canada. He finally had the chance to observe his father closely and learn how to be

Wong Gay Sieng, Ah Dang's adoptive father, *circa* 1920s.

an honourable man, but the time they spent together was cut cruelly short. Just a few years after welcoming his son to Canada, Ah Gay Sieng took his final trip back to China. Only in his fourth decade of life, he had been diagnosed with throat cancer. Back home, sensing he had little time left, he wrote to his son, requesting him to return to China to choose a bride. Sadly, Ah Gay Sieng did not live to see this final wish fulfilled. Ah Dang was now the keeper of the family line.

[W]eeding their fields by hand, crawling between their crops on
their hands and knees with the sun roasting their backs and the
mud soaking their limbs—[was] a truly pitiable fate . . .
                    —Francesca Bray, *The Rice Economies:*
            Technology and Development in Asian Societies

TWO
Hai Ngao Nui—*Cowherd Girl*

AH THLOO: CHINA, 1921

"Hurry up! Move, you stubborn old bull! Time to go home. It's my turn
to eat." The buffalo didn't move, despite the tug on its nose and the bare
heels beating rhythmically on its flank. Ten-year-old Ah Thloo fearlessly
straddled its back. She was a small girl, but for her age and size, she was
strong. *Thwack! Thwack! Thwack!* The bamboo switch she held in her other
hand slapped the animal's rump, urging it to stop grazing and start walking. However, none of her kicks or slaps hurt the animal. She would never
do anything to jeopardize the health of the buffalo, for it was her family's
most valuable asset.

o   o   o

AH THLOO'S FAMILY: CHINA, 1877–1925

Ah Thloo always said she came from humble beginnings. "My parents were
just farming peasants and I was a *hai ngao nui*, cowherd girl."

Her family had grown rice and vegetables on leased lands for generations. Of her parents, it was her mother, whom she called Ah Ma, who was

the farmer, responsible for the fields, overseeing seasonal helpers, and toiling on the land herself. The family also kept chickens, geese, ducks, and pigs.

It was her father, whom she called Ah Yea, who was the exception. Unlike most of their neighbours in the large, rural village of Ngao Loo How in Guangdong Province, Ah Thloo's father, Jiang Poy Lim, had been educated and did not actually work the land. He was born in the third year of Emperor Guangxu's reign, in 1877, on the seventh day of the eleventh month of the lunar calendar. An experienced architect and builder, he often lived on-site at construction projects in neighbouring towns and villages. Well known around the county for his skill as well as his honesty in business dealings, he prospered for a time. He insisted on being paid in *tien*, cash; he provided an allowance to his wife to purchase necessities and left the running of the household to his mother and the farming to his wife and children.

With prudent money management, Ah Poy Lim's wife invested in land, but these were only small, scattered plots, worked on by the household's members. Thus, the Jiang family was never known as *aye jee*, landlords. Ah Poy Lim's work brought in cash, but like the cobbler's children who are the last to get shoes, his family had to make do with limited space in their home. He just never got around to expanding his own, three-room house.

To his family, he was a remote but kindly figure. During the days when he was not on a job, he sat at a teahouse in the neighbouring market town of Vak Sa, passing the time over a pot of tea, exchanging news, and conducting business with other men. He came home just to eat his meals and to sleep.

At dinner, Ah Poy Lim was served first. Only after he had swallowed a final bowl of clear broth, and emitted a loud belch to show his appreciation of the meal, did the rest of the family eat. No one in the family thought this practice was strange; it was just the way things were and always had been.

When Ah Poy Lim came home from his jobs, the house took on a different atmosphere, like that of a festival day. The servant girls, daughters of poor relatives, made sure every corner of the house was spotless and all the rooms were aired. Ah Poy Lim always brought home treats for his dinner and was generous in sharing them with the family. From the kitchen hearth came the pungent smells of dried salted fish, fermented shrimp paste, or pressed goose.

He was a traditionalist in other ways. While he valued education, he saw its benefits only for his sons. His eldest son, Gim Yoke, received a superior education, and Ah Poy Lim was progressive enough to allow the young man to study art at a Western university in distant Shanghai. Ah Thloo would later recall sneaking into her older brother's room one day and being embarrassed, but fascinated, at discovering drawings he had done of naked women.

When Ah Thloo was born, on the eleventh day of the first month of the lunar calendar, in 1911, the country was just getting over the disastrous effects of the 1907 famine in east-central China, which had extinguished twenty-four million lives. Although the disaster had occurred a thousand kilometres north of the family's farm, starving refugees drifted south into Guangdong Province and food riots broke out in its capital city, Guangzhou. In addition, political forces were on the brink of toppling the last emperor of the Qing Dynasty, the child P'u-i, who lived in distant Beijing. A change in the Mandate of Heaven could only bring chaos. When her father named her Tew Thloo, meaning "Autumn Compassion," he hoped that the chaos would be short-lived. Unfortunately, it was not.

Guangzhou's newspapers followed the exploits of its star citizen, Dr. Sun Yat-sen, who became China's first president on January 1, 1912. He provided China's people with their first brief taste of democracy. A month later, Dr. Sun resigned in favour of General Yuan Shikai, the former leader of the Imperial troops, in an attempt to maintain harmony within the country and to protect it against foreign intervention. The general, an experienced military organizer and diplomat, also known as a reformer, was thought to be the right choice as president, but declaring himself president for life, Yuan actually aspired to become the next emperor. Although he never succeeded in crowning himself, he ruled as if he had, through a brief reign of political terror, until his sudden demise in 1916.

Living in Ngao Loo How, a few days' travel south of Guangzhou, far away from the battlefields and centres of political intrigue in Beijing, Ah Thloo and her family were sheltered from direct danger for much of her childhood. The seasons, more than politics, ruled their daily lives. Surrounded by bamboo forests, fields, and rice paddies, they spent their days coaxing sustenance from the soil.

In the years when the weather gods smiled—rather than cursing people with floods or droughts—vegetables, fruits, and sugar cane grew in abundance. Silkworms thrived in mulberry fields. But the most important of all the crops was rice, the symbol of life. At every meal, Ah Thloo and her siblings were reminded of its preciousness and dared not leave a single grain uneaten in their bowls. Their mantra was "one grain of rice is one drop of sweat."

The rice-growing cycle started with the monsoons, when rainwater made it possible for the fields to be broken up and the soil mixed into a thick, smooth mud. It was helpful to have a water buffalo to pull a plow; otherwise, tilling and churning were done by hand-held tools and stomping feet. Sprouted rice shoots were transplanted by hand into rows in the newly prepared fields.

The shoots grew in standing water, while human-powered irrigation wheels adjusted the water levels. Night soil, the black gold of peasant farmers, fertilized the crop. After a few months, the water was drained away, and the mature stalks were cut by hand and stacked upright in bunches to dry. Then the stalks were threshed, the kernels spread out in the sun, and the husks ground off. Finally, the precious pearls were gathered and stored in airtight ceramic jars. Each step required a large investment of human labour, and everyone in the family was expected to work and contribute to the household's efforts.

The Jiang family's traditional living arrangements facilitated this; sharing the three-room house were Ah Thloo's paternal grandmother, parents, older brother and his wife, and two older sisters. Ah Thloo's mother was a tall, handsome woman. Originally of the Loo family, Ah Shee had been born on the third day of the tenth month of the lunar calendar in 1880. Over her lifetime, Ah Shee bore six children, but only five survived to adulthood. Her first-born, a girl they named Tew Fuy, died young. Her next child, the son, Gim Yoke, on whom everyone doted, was born in 1899. Then followed three daughters: Tew May in 1901, Tew Ngoke in 1905, and Tew Thloo in 1911.

Ah Shee, like her husband, had never been demonstrative with her children; her days, which started before dawn and ended long after sundown, were too filled with physical toil to allow time for play. Of course, she had nursed them when they were younger, carrying them in a *via aie*, a baby sling, when she went to work in the fields. The carrier, a square piece of fabric with four long cloth straps, secured the baby with its belly on her back while she worked and provided a snug holder in front for the child while she breast-fed. She had nursed her first son for as long as he wanted; she had been young and strong. The rest of the children were weaned after six months and left in the care of their paternal grandmother. When the youngsters were old enough to feed themselves and walk unaided, and were deemed to have enough dexterity to pull weeds, they accompanied her to the fields. Every hand, no matter how small, was needed for the work.

By the time Ah Shee's youngest and last son, Ngien Choo, was born in 1918, her two eldest children were married. A year later, her third daughter was married off to a man from Southeast Asia. Her son had brought his wife home, and her daughters had gone to live with their respective parents-in-law. The girls had been good helpers around the house and fields, and with them gone, the Jiang family had to sublet their leased lands.

Ah Shee had a caring, if distant, relationship with her daughters. A parent rarely grew too emotionally attached to a daughter because she was destined to belong to another family. If time, distance, and their mothers-in-law allowed, Ah Shee's daughters were encouraged to come back with the grandchildren to visit once a year during Gwoh Nien, the fifteen-day New Year festival. To celebrate, the extended family took a few afternoons off work and gathered for feasting; no farmer could afford to leave the crops for two whole weeks.

Ah Thloo remembered her sisters bringing gifts of homemade *dim sum*—small, sweet or savoury dumplings—live geese, fruits, and sweets. Sugar cane stalks were a favourite. Once the hard outer bark was shaved away with a knife, the fibrous tissues of the stalk could be cut into bite-sized rounds for the children. Adults tore chunks directly off the stalk with their teeth and chewed to release the subtly sweet juice, spitting the remains onto the ground. As the day wore on, the broken, dried fibres piled up in front of everyone's feet. The mounds were then gathered into a bucket and used as pig feed; nothing was wasted.

Ah Thloo's family was luckier than most, as her father's earnings had enabled the family to purchase their own water buffalo. Landowners of large holdings had most of the other beasts of burden in the village. Without the animal, Ah Thloo's family could not have managed the extra fields they owned and would have grown only enough to feed themselves. They would not have had any surplus to trade for luxuries like salt, tea, and tobacco nor could they have afforded to take a few afternoons off to celebrate the holiday. Those who could afford it leased a buffalo, sometimes from their mother.

Ah Thloo also considered herself luckier than most children, for she had a best friend in the family's water buffalo. She thought often of the day she was introduced to him.

Jiang Tew Ngoke, AKA Ah Thlam Day, in her latter years, 1966.
ROBERT WONG, CHINA

Ah Thloo was only six at the time, but she understood how important the animal was, and approached him reverently and cautiously. He towered over her, but she trusted her elder sister, who showed no fear as she stood between Ah Thloo and the buffalo. After all, Tew Ngoke, whom she called Ah Thlam Day, Third Elder Sister, was his minder, a *hai ngao nui*. She was also Ah Thloo's idol.

Just as Ah Thloo's trembling fingers reached up to touch the yellow bristles around the buffalo's mouth, he shook his head and snorted. Stepping back to avoid the spray of warm, gooey snot, too late to close her mouth, she fell, sputtering and spitting. "Echhh!"

"Ha! Ha! Ha! He did the same thing the first time I met him! He's saying, 'How are you?'" her older sister said, bent over with laughter.

When Ah Thloo picked herself up from the ground after being "greeted" by the water buffalo, she offered him a handful of fresh grass.

"It's his favourite! You can call him Ah Ngao," Ah Ngoke approved.

A few days later, Ah Thloo had her first ride. Holding on to the reins, Ah Ngoke gave her a boost onto the buffalo's broad back.

"Sit right behind the hump on his back. Press your legs tightly on each side. Don't worry, his horns can't reach you there, even when he turns his head."

Stepping onto a stump, the older girl grasped one horn and, using the animal's shoulder muscles as footholds for her bare feet, climbed on behind her sister. Ah Thloo trembled with excitement, but her delight turned to fear when the animal started to walk and she was thrown off balance. Ah Ngoke caught her and hugged her close, whispering, "You are so brave!"

The buffalo took them along one of the paths circling the rice paddies. By the time they reached their home, Ah Thloo's body had learned to sway with the buffalo's movements and she was balancing on her own. The dilemma of how to get off was solved when her sister dismounted first and caught Ah Thloo as she slid off. Although her thighs ached and her legs shook like jelly, she hobbled into the house to announce her triumphant first buffalo ride to her mother and grandmother.

Over the next few weeks, Ah Thloo learned to mount and dismount on her own. If her buttocks became numb while riding, she discovered she could move and shift her body without causing the animal to miss a stride. Her sister taught her the verbal commands and the non-verbal cues: a tug on the reins, a nudge of the thighs, or a flick of the bamboo switch. Ah Thloo learned that despite the buffalo's size and imposing, sharp, curved horns, it was quite docile around people. Sometimes, her sister just held on to its tail and walked alongside; it knew the way home.

Although they were separated by six years, Ah Thloo and her sister were very similar. Unlike their tall mother and older siblings, both girls were compact. They did things slowly and methodically, speaking quietly, but with hidden strength. That was probably why the water buffalo adjusted so quickly to Ah Thloo. Not long afterwards, her sister told her, "Ah Thloo, you have learned your lessons well. You will now take care of Ah Ngao. Mother needs me to work in the fields."

Later that year, Ah Ngoke moved to the *nui oak*, girls' house, a few lanes from their own home. Ah Thloo was torn between losing her sister's companionship and looking forward to her new responsibility and its accompanying freedom. The paths of the two sisters naturally diverged, but the bonds they had shared while looking after Ah Ngao served to keep them close.

o   o   o

AH THLOO: CHINA, 1921

Four years after Ah Thloo's meeting with Ah Ngao, Ah Ngoke had married and moved away, and her baby brother had been born. In addition to Ah Thloo's main job as a cowherd, she was responsible for taking care of her brother in the evenings.

Recently, she had joined a small group of other cowherds, all children of landless peasants who were hired to watch their charges in exchange for an evening meal from the respective animals' owners. Their brief company in the mornings, and occasionally at midday, relieved the monotony of her job. Ah Thloo's own bull, while castrated, apparently retained some residual testosterone, and when another one came near, an inevitable show of domination occurred. With a member of the opposite sex, the mêlée that ensued could be worse. The animal had to be kept apart from the others; buffalo-minding was a lonely job.

Each morning, after completing her household chores, Ah Thloo ate a meagre meal—often just a cup of hot tea and a small bowl of *jook*, rice soup, flavoured with leftovers from the previous night's supper. The children met when they fetched their animals from the communal byre. Unlike Ah Thloo, few of the other children had eaten anything, so they organized garden raids to feed themselves. Ah Thloo knew it was wrong to steal, but she participated to help her companions. Depending on what the children planned to take and whether it required cooking, they each took certain responsibilities on a rotating basis. These jobs included the scout, who suggested the targeted garden and a safe place to gather, the robbers, and the cook, who was also the lookout.

One day, when it was Ah Thloo's turn to be a raider, the group had chosen the garden of an old crone nicknamed Woo Diek Na, "Screeching Crow." Her reputation as the meanest woman in the village was as long and legendary as the Great Wall. A rich widow with painful bound feet, she tyrannized her family with her scorching tongue and a ready whip of willow branches. She terrorized the servants and screeched at anyone who passed by her door. She hated children; it was rumoured she ate them as a snack. But her garden grew the largest and sweetest yams around. The old woman left the gardening to servants but occasionally surveyed her holdings, and she arrived, carried on a two-person sedan chair, just as the children were pulling the last yellow root out of the ground at the far end of the plot.

"*Aiya!* Thieves!" Ah Woo Diek Na shrieked, waving her whip above her head. "You are dead ghosts!" She slapped the front sedan carrier. "Run faster, you lazy turtle! I'll chop your heads off, you dead kids!"

They might have caught up to the children—if the old woman had stopped jostling the chair, if the front carrier hadn't kept closing his eyes for fear of losing them to the whip, and if the back carrier hadn't caught his feet on the roots sticking up from the newly turned soil. *Splat!* Landing face down on a pile of manure collected as fertilizer, the old crone was abruptly, effectively silenced.

Now it was evening and time to go home. Chuckling at the memory, Ah Thloo also shuddered at their close encounter. But if they hadn't taken the chance, her companions would have had nothing to eat until late in the day. She had taken only a small piece to be polite and had shared her own light lunch. For this particular day's lunch, her grandmother had wrapped six cold, litchi-sized balls of rice, flavoured with dabs of shrimp paste, in a bamboo leaf.

The hot, sweet, forbidden yam had been all the more delicious, and her stomach now chortled, not with mirth but in renewed hunger.

Strands of her long, jet-black hair, which had been tightly braided that morning, stuck to her face. With a few deft twists, she rebraided it and bound it with twine to create a loop, keeping it off her neck. Working the twine reminded her of the neat, tasty parcels of *donge*, large, rice-based dumplings, which her grandmother had wrapped and tied that morning to celebrate the Dragon Boat Festival.

Ah Ngange, Father's mother, had been making preparations over the past few days. She had bought, seasoned, and soaked the special glutinous rice; sorted and soaked dried bamboo leaves; and cleaned, chopped, and marinated the other ingredients that had been carefully hoarded for the occasion. The filling included sausage, marinated pork, pieces of mushroom, salted duck egg yolks, and peanuts.

The bamboo leaves were used to form a pouch. One wet, supple bamboo leaf was folded into a shovel and into it the ingredients were layered between spoonfuls of raw rice, filling it about halfway. Another leaf was folded to enclose the side, and the two upper halves were folded over from the top to cover the filling. A string was wound horizontally and vertically to secure the package, which was shaped like a double pyramid.

Dumped into large pots of water, the dumplings simmered for hours over a coal fire. The packages would swell between the strings as the rice cooked, and when their texture changed from hard to pliable, as tested by Ah Ngange's seemingly heat-immune bare fingers, they were scooped out of the pots with a long-handled colander made from a coconut shell. Her grandmother always added a special treat for Ah Thloo in the donge, identifying them with a special knot of the twine. They would be ready to eat by the time the girl got home at sundown.

Ah Thloo could almost feel the warm, firm parcel in her hand as she imagined cutting the twine that bound the fragrant bamboo leaves. Inside, she would find a whole salted duck egg yolk, instead of the usual half. She knew what she would bring for lunch the next day and enjoyed the anticipation of sharing it with her companions. The thought made her stomach rumble loudly and her mouth water hungrily.

She repeated her urgings to Ah Ngao: "Come on, you lazy thing! You've been wandering the countryside eating all day. Now it's my turn, and I'm hungry for donge. Let's go home! You are an ugly, stubborn old thing, but you are my true friend." She smiled at what she had just said. Perhaps it was silly, thinking about a water buffalo that way, but what *was* a friend? She had learned it was someone who spent time with you, listened to everything you said without arguing or dismissing your opinions, never told your secrets to anyone else, and never hurt you.

In all the years she had looked after the animal, she had never been bitten, gored, kicked, stepped on, or thrown off its back. Ah Ngao had always been gentle with Ah Thloo, and always—eventually—responded to her directions and exhortations. Slowly, he turned his head and body in the direction of the village and lumbered forward.

"*Oo deah*, thank you, Ah Ngao!"

She did not consider the other cowherds to be her friends, especially not the boys—they always thought they were superior to her. She could not talk to them the same way she talked to Ah Ngao, but she would enjoy their brief, joint adventures for now. They would soon separate, for the time was drawing near for her to move to the nui oak, the mysterious place where girls became women and left to become wives.

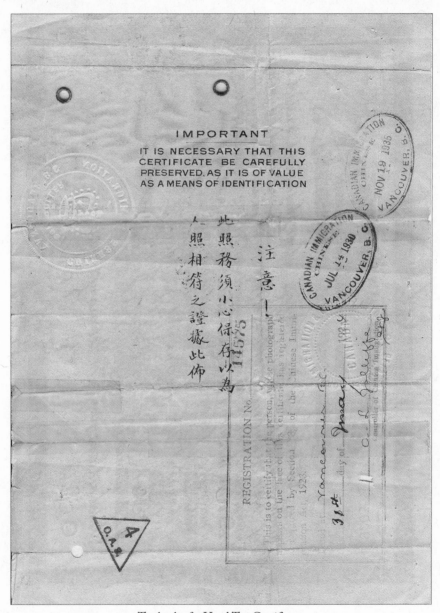

IMPORTANT

IT IS NECESSARY THAT THIS
CERTIFICATE BE CAREFULLY
PRESERVED, AS IT IS OF VALUE
AS A MEANS OF IDENTIFICATION

注意！

此照務須小心保存以為
人照相符之證據此佈

CANADIAN IMMIGRATION
CHINESE
NOV 19 1935
VANCOUVER, B.C.

CANADIAN IMMIGRATION
CHINESE
JUL 14 1930
VANCOUVER, B.C.

REGISTRATION No. 14575

This is to certify that the person, whose photograph
is on the face of this certificate has registered
as required by Section 18 of the Chinese Immigration Act, 1923.

Vancouver B.C.

31st day of January 192

O. L. Lewis
Controller of Chinese Immigration

The back of a Head Tax Certificate.

Since 1885 Canada, and particularly British Columbia, has been faced with the problem of Oriental immigration—especially Chinese, Japanese and East Indian. The objections to Orientals is not so much racial, social, or religious, as chiefly economic; accustomed as they are to long hours, low wages, and a low standard of living, the Asiatics are able to underbid the white man in selling his labour.

—Stewart W. Wallace, editor, *Encyclopaedia of Canada*

THREE
Father Reborn

The head tax receipt was more than a proof of payment, a certificate of immigration, or a passport: any Royal Canadian Mounted Police or immigration officer could, at any time and place, demand to see this document. A failure to produce it immediately might be cause for incarceration or deportation. Measuring approximately eight and a half by eleven inches, it was not an insignificant piece of identification to carry around.

o o o

AH DANG: CANADA, 1921–1923

Ah Dang sailed to Canada on the once-famous *Empress of Japan*. When it was launched in 1891 to deliver mail between Britain and Canada, the 148-metre ship was a model of efficiency, speed, and elegance. During the voyage, as he watched, listened to, and sometimes chatted with the many Chinese crew working on board as stewards and kitchen and laundry staff, Ah Dang learned about its illustrious history and current capacity.

In 1897, the ship had set a speed record for the North Pacific, sailing thirteen hundred kilometres in only ten days. It had served as a luxury liner, cargo ship, and even an armed First World War merchant cruiser carrying Chinese labourers to and from the Western Front. It had transported cargoes of tea, silk, opium, and general merchandise, but the company that owned the ship made the bulk of its money from the passengers in Asiatic steerage.

By the time Ah Dang sailed on the ship, it was far past its prime. He travelled with a distant cousin from his hamlet, a nephew of Ah Ngay Gonge, his father's benefactor. On September 20, 1921, the teens boarded the ship in Hong Kong. It stopped in Shanghai, Kobe, and Yokohama before arriving in Vancouver on October 10, 1921, taking twice as long to complete this shorter trip as it had during its heyday. Unfortunately for its passengers, the ship was not known for its stability, and rolled heavily in rough weather. Since the route took it through the North Pacific, past the Aleutian Islands toward Vancouver, gale-force winds, rough seas, and ice tested the constitutions of all on board during that fall crossing.

Advertisements had once extolled the fabulous amenities offered by the *Empress of Japan*. For the thirty-one saloon or first-class passengers on that trip, Ah Dang learned, the ship was still a luxurious floating palace, providing the best in furnishings, comfort, and food. Meals apparently offered a different daily assortment of foods, with foreign names like hors d'oeuvres, salmon, cheese, coffee, and wine.

While boarding, Ah Dang had stolen glimpses of the staterooms, equipped with beds, chairs, and individual electrical fans. He and his Chinese compatriots were hurried past covered promenades, with comfortable chairs and tables between potted palms. He never got to see the dining saloon, which the stewards described as having coloured-glass windows, its walls covered in silk, and floors made of smooth, polished wood.

Ah Dang and his cousin had accommodations in an open berth at one end of the main deck. These sparsely furnished cargo areas were designated solely for Chinese, Japanese, and other Asiatic men. At one time, the ship could carry up to seven hundred such passengers, spread throughout the two lower decks, but Ah Dang and his cousin shared the main deck compartment with only a hundred and ten others.

In contrast to what he heard about the food for first-class passengers,

Ah Dang and his travelling companions were offered the same meal of rice mixed with meagre bits of thlonge, day in and day out. It was not very tasty, and the helpings were small. However, they soon learned that the *real* food would arrive late in the evening, delivered by the kitchen staff. For about twenty cents a bowl, they could buy rice cooked with aromatic Chinese sausage or salted duck eggs. Between the two teens, they occasionally splurged and bought a couple of bowls of this Chinese comfort food, hoping to get information from the staff about the ship and, most importantly, about their destination.

When the ship landed in Vancouver, the upper-deck passengers alighted at their leisure while the steerage passengers were counted. At last, they too disembarked, but they were herded like prisoners directly to an immigration building at the bottom of Burrard Street, known to the Chinese as the "Pig Pen." On board, they had been warned about having to wait in this no man's land until their papers were verified, the five-hundred-dollar head tax was paid, and a picture was taken for their identity document. The process could take months. No one knew the reason for the delays, but everyone who had been through it was convinced that the Chinese interpreters were waiting to be paid graft before processing any new immigrants.

The boys were ready to watch each other's backs and their few personal belongings. At the immigration station, they were held behind locked doors among frustrated, angry men and boys, already fed up with waiting, who fought to secure their daily rations of bread and sugar. They were each assigned a metal bed; they had to wrap their quilts around themselves to do double duty as mattress and blanket.

Taking in his surroundings, Ah Dang couldn't help but notice that the walls were covered in Chinese characters, some carved, some elegantly painted in ink, some written in crude, dark strokes the colour of dried blood. One quote in particular echoed his own thoughts: "I have always yearned to reach the Golden Mountain. But instead, it is hell, full of hardship. I was detained in a prison ... Who can foretell when I will be able to return home? March, 1919."

Ah Dang spent his nineteenth birthday behind bars. October to February were four months of confinement and starvation in a cold, dank, dreary building in a chilly, damp, rain-drenched city by the sea. Who would have believed it of Gold Mountain?

NUMBER
92036

DOMINION

IMMIGRATION BRANCH —

RECEIV

Wong Guey Da

hereto, on the date and at the p
of Five Hundred Dollars
provisions of the Chinese Imm
The above mentioned party who
a native of *Wong hai*
in the District of Hoi
of the age of 19 years arrive
at Vancouver on the 10
October 1921 ex Emp
The declaration in this case is 61

Dated at Vancouver on Febru

CONTROLLE

BRITISH AMERI

Ah Dang's Head Tax Certificate.

OF CANADA

RTMENT OF THE INTERIOR

FROM

whose photograph is attached
hereunder mentioned, the sum
ng the head tax due under the
ation Act.
ims to be

oo

ing

anded

day of

Japan

37297

721 1922

NESE IMMIGRATION

E C° OTTAWA.

Once the head tax money was paid, the immigration office issued a receipt and the individual was allowed to "land" and enter Canada. Finally, the call came for Ah Dang to have his photograph taken. Knowing this was the final step before he would be released and reunited with his father, he dressed carefully in the Western clothing Ah Gay Sieng had sent for the journey. It included a dark tie, patterned with butterflies on a field of small flower petals. In the portrait, his eyes look directly at the camera, as if in challenge. Some people still look innocent at nineteen, but Ah Dang had lost his innocence in childhood. Did his hard, cold eyes reflect his indifference or perhaps his readiness to face the coming difficulties of living in a foreign land that did not want him?

With his head tax paper, Ah Dang reinvented himself once more; he officially existed in a way that he had not in his homeland. The Canadian officials anglicized his Chinese name, Wong Guey Dang, by writing it phonetically in English. With the recording of his birth date, he was reborn, for he had no previous records from China that verified his being. This was his passport to a new life.

Ah Dang had landed. The form he held in his hands was definitive proof, his receipt for the price of admission to Gold Mountain. His father, Ah Gay Sieng, had paid the five hundred dollars, an exorbitantly high cost in many ways. Back then, the amount would have bought two houses in Canada. It would have been more than enough to build a mansion in China for Ah Tew May, his wife, to live the rest of her life in splendour, but instead he used it to buy his adopted son's way into Canada. When Ah Tew May learned of her husband's intentions, she had additional reasons to resent the boy.

○   ○   ○   ·

Why did the Chinese so willingly pay such a high price to leave China? Most would say, "To make a better life for my family." There was a century-long mass emigration from China between 1849 and 1949, known as the Chinese Diaspora.

Through most of the eighteenth century, China enjoyed an economic boom—the country was self-sufficient and a trade surplus existed. The exports of highly sought-after teas, silks, porcelain, and other Chinese decorative items far outweighed the imports of European and American goods. Chinese merchants, farmers, and manufacturers prospered, along with the national coffers.

Alarmed at the mounting deficit, British and American merchants devised a strategy to import opium from the British colonies in India into China in the 1760s. The drug was easily accessible, and a growing proportion of the nation, in all parts of society, became addicted, until the trade imbalance was reversed. Silver, the currency of international commerce, was drained from China. While the Chinese government tried to curb the addiction problem by banning the import, production, and smoking of opium, British and American merchants continued to smuggle it in, in cooperation with unscrupulous Chinese officials and criminals.

When the Chinese government legally destroyed a shipment of contraband opium in Guangzhou in 1839, Britain declared war. China's inevitable loss in the First Opium War virtually crushed the independence of the nation. It had to submit to crippling indemnity payments in silver and the granting of excessive demands. Borders were forcibly opened to foreign missionaries. The principle of extraterritoriality was extended, exempting all Westerners from the laws of China, no matter the seriousness of their crimes. Hong Kong Island was ceded to Britain. Other treaty ports, like the one in Guangzhou, were established in Amoy, Fuzhou, Shanghai, and Ningpo. Unfortunately, this pattern—aggression, China's defeat, and its concessions to foreign victors—was to occur a number of times over the next century.

The burden of indemnity had a trickle-down effect, which fell heavily on the peasant farmers. As the largest sector of the population, they bore the brunt of the taxation. Although the value of bank notes fell against the rise in the value of silver being drained from the national treasury, the level of taxation on harvests remained the same.

Some peasant farmers might have owned land, but most paid for the use of leased land with a percentage of whatever they harvested. Only aye jee, landlords, with their ability to collect rents and sell large amounts of produce (collected from their various tenants), made money.

With the devaluation of silver, landlords required higher payments, demanding up to half of the crops. Tenants descended further in arrears through borrowing at usurious rates, some as high as 30 per cent for six months. As the debts rose, bankrupted peasants eventually lost whatever land they had leased, while landowners took advantage of their increasing liabilities and amassed more and more property. Peasant farmers were major participants in the mass exodus from China.

Overpopulation in South China was another driver of emigration. Along the coast of East Guangdong, a population of more than four million people occupied an area of just under four thousand, five hundred square miles. This was almost nine hundred persons per square mile, and some areas had even higher densities. Since the local population grew all its own food, this level of crowding was unsustainable.

Peasants rebelled against the high taxes and increasing poverty. To escape the unrest, uncertainty, and unbearable burdens, migrants left China in record numbers, estimated at fifteen million or more.

Their move to North America came in waves, starting with the United States. The California Gold Rush of 1849 sparked the first wave, drawing more than twenty thousand Chinese to California by 1852. The first Chinese came to Canada via the United States, and when gold was discovered in the lower Fraser River in British Columbia in 1858, large numbers came directly from China. By 1879, some four thousand Chinese were living in the province, more than half of whom had settled in Victoria's Chinatown.

The building of the westernmost section of the Canadian Pacific Railway brought the next wave of Chinese immigration. Chinese workers, who had built the American railways, had earned the reputation of being willing, reliable, and industrious; more than fifteen thousand were recruited between 1880 and 1885.

It was treacherous and dangerous work. The Chinese, with their smaller statures that enabled them to crawl into cramped spaces, were sought after to lay blasting materials for only marginally higher pay. Living in makeshift tents along the route of the railroad, hundreds died from cold winter conditions, malnutrition, sickness, and accidents. The construction company estimated that at least six hundred Chinese workers died, or more than four workers for every mile of track laid along that part. The Chinese worked for less than half the going rate paid to white workers, and it has been estimated that hiring Chinese workers saved the government three and a half million dollars. Due to the workers' work ethic, tenacity, and ingenuity, the railroad was completed five years ahead of schedule.

But the completion of the railroad meant that Chinese workers were no longer needed in Canada. Thousands returned to China, but many stayed, even though they could not easily find jobs. The country was undergoing a time of economic slowdown, and with increasing unemployment, white workers were afraid the Chinese would, by accepting lower wages, take scarce jobs away.

As economic conditions worsened, so did overt discrimination and racism against the Chinese. They were taunted and harassed by individual citizens, assaulted by mobs, and publicly denounced by community leaders. At every level of government, legal steps were taken to "regulate the Chinese population."

In 1885, the Dominion Government passed the Chinese Immigration Act, imposing a fifty-dollar head tax for every Chinese immigrant entering Canada. The weight of the tax was enormous. By 1900, the Chinese had entered new occupations such as operating laundries, market gardens, and inexpensive restaurants.

Although they prospered, many immigrants could still not afford to bring their families from China. As was tradition, they sent remittances to support their relatives and home communities, in addition to making sporadic visits; thus they were called "sojourners." Their habits of living alone with no families—"They must be morally depraved!"—and their sending money out of the country—"They don't support our local economy!"—were used as justifications by the white establishment to continue discriminatory practices. Labour unions and politicians in BC were particularly strident in lobbying for federal laws to further limit Oriental immigration.

The Dominion Government passed a new Chinese Immigration Act, enacted on June 1, 1902, doubling the existing head tax to one hundred dollars. To appease BC, which had lobbied for a five-hundred-dollar tax, the federal government allowed the province to retain half the proceeds of the hundred-dollar fee. Ships carrying Chinese immigrants were limited to one person per fifty tonnes of cargo, or risked a fine. Still, the province continued to agitate for more restrictions. One outcome was the establishment of a royal commission, which concluded that the continuing policy of limiting immigration from China would not adversely affect trade between that country and Canada. However, the increased tax did not deter immigration either, and the number of new arrivals remained similar to previous years, averaging two thousand people per year.

In 1903, the head tax was once again increased. Set at five hundred dollars, it was equivalent to two years of work at white man's wages. As before, only the Chinese were required to pay. On July 1, 1923, another Chinese Immigration Act came into effect. A response to growing anti-Oriental sentiment arising out of the post-war economic collapse, the act virtually shut down further Chinese immigration, with the exception of university students, merchants (except anyone involved in laundries, restaurants, or retail produce), Canadian-born Chinese, and diplomatic personnel. On the positive side, the head tax was finally abolished.

The Chinese community living in Canada was stunned by the far-reaching implications. The people felt betrayed by the country that they had helped to build, through the sacrifice of their devalued labour and lives. On subsequent Dominion Days, when the rest of Canada celebrated, the Chinese mourned it as "Humiliation Day" until the act was finally abolished in 1947.

Between 1885 and 1923, an estimated twenty-three million dollars was collected from the head tax. During this period, young men, and the families and villages who supported their bid for a better life, still found it worthwhile to try their luck in Canada. At home in their villages, they might have found enough work to earn two dollars a month; in Canada, they could earn ten times that amount, money they could remit back to their families.

In BC, laws were passed that denied the Chinese the right to vote, to own land, and to work on Crown land or on provincial projects. Since they were not on the voters list, Chinese could not work in the professions. Even with proper and otherwise accepted credentials, they could not practise law or be accountants or pharmacists.

Following the railway, the Chinese moved east, hoping to find less discrimination and more work. They settled in communities like Calgary, Moose Jaw, and Regina, eventually reaching Winnipeg, Toronto, and Montreal.

As Ah Dang later discovered, Chinatowns might have been created out of preference but they were maintained out of necessity. The Chinese congregated to form a community, but governments and white residents also preferred them to be segregated. The largest Chinatowns in BC were in Vancouver, Victoria, New Westminster, and Nanaimo, and in the rest of Canada in Calgary, Toronto, and Montreal.

By 1911, there were almost twenty-eight thousand Chinese in Canada, of whom 71 per cent lived in BC, 10 per cent in Ontario, and about 6 per cent each in Alberta and Quebec. By 1921, there were almost forty thousand Chinese, 60 per cent of whom lived in BC.

But the 1920s also saw the start of growing interaction with whites and changing attitudes, some for the better. A few years after Ah Dang arrived, the Vancouver Chinese Students Athletic Club, featuring star player Quene Yip, joined the city soccer league and held its own against white teams. In 1933, when the Chinese team won the BC Soccer Championship, all of Chinatown celebrated the victory.

o   o   o

A number of significant events that took place in China between 1916 and 1928, although they did not directly involve Ah Thloo or Ah Dang, did eventually have an effect on their social, economic, and political environment.

The sudden death of President Yuan Shikai in 1916 plunged the country into what was called the Warlord Period until 1928. Autonomous warlords, many of whom were regional governors with private armies, ruled their kingdoms more through coercion than statecraft. Warlords maintained individual power and authority through the creation of alliances, and as loyalties shifted, wars broke out. Opposing armies relied on the local peasantry for new recruits, as well as to feed, house, and care for them, thus terrorizing the countryside. The shout of "Bandits are coming!" was a warning cry for Ah Thloo and her family to get home behind barred doors.

As an enticement for China to assist Britain against Germany in the First World War, a promise was made that German-occupied Chinese lands, especially on the strategically important coast of Shandong Province, would be returned after the war. However, the 1919 Treaty of Versailles gave the territories to Japan, an old enemy. This decision was seen by the Chinese people as a betrayal and a humiliation of China at the hands of foreign imperialist powers, and galvanized thousands of patriotic students, union workers, and even merchants to protest at Tiananmen Square in Beijing, on May 4, 1919. The May Fourth Movement showed that all levels of citizenry, including peasant farmers who protested against landlords, could be mobilized for a nationalist cause.

The Chinese Communist Party (CCP) was officially founded in 1921, in Shanghai, but did not gain popularity until 1925. In 1923, Dr. Sun Yat-sen again came into the limelight, at the head of a reorganized Kuomintang (KMT) Party, and established the Nationalist Government in Guangzhou in 1924. His intention was to defeat the warlords and take up the call for nationalism by ridding the country of foreign concessions and privileges. Dr. Sun created a strategic alliance with the CCP and invited Soviet advisers to build an army to fight the warlords and to train the Chinese in how to mobilize the masses. Two key figures emerged at this time: Jiang Jieshi, representing the KMT, and Zhou Enlai, representing the CPP, and both took on important roles at the newly created Whampoa Military Academy.

Dr. Sun died of cancer in March 1925. On May 30 of that year, a student demonstration in the Shanghai International Settlement, which culminated in a British police commander and his mainly Sikh officers shooting and killing Chinese protesters, triggered another nationwide outcry against foreigners. In Guangzhou, merchants recruited their own armies to enforce a fifteen-month strike and boycott of British goods. These events boosted membership in the CCP to twenty thousand and led to the creation of units responsible for peasants, women, labour, and military affairs.

In 1926, General Jiang Jieshi led the Northern Expedition from Guangzhou to fight the warlords and unify China and met with success in southern China. The fragile alliance between the KMT and CPP broke apart in 1927, when Jiang used his Shanghai underworld gang connections to seek out and destroy Chinese Communists. General Jiang took over the leadership of the KMT and set up a politically right-wing Nationalist government in Nanjing in 1928.

In Canada, the Chinese-Canadian community was very politically involved, divided along the same lines as in China, but there was hope that the KMT Nationalist government would bring stability. Chinese Canadians in leadership positions in the KMT Party in Canada were recognized as being linked to the new government in China. When a KMT convention was held at the Empress Hotel in Victoria, the party reached out to local leaders, inviting the premier and his cabinet, the mayor and aldermen, the American consul, and the head of the Chamber of Commerce, as well as service club and business leaders to a banquet.

A Canadian Trade Commission office was established in Shanghai, and by 1926, Canada had started sending trade missions. Canada exported wheat, flour, timber, clothing, electrical appliances, machinery, and foods to China. Canadian insurance and shipping companies were established in China. Almost seventy years after the first Chinese immigrants landed in Canada, improvements could finally be seen at some key levels of Chinese-Canadian relations.

o   o   o

AH DANG: CHINA, 1929

For reasons now lost in time, Ah Dang couldn't get back to China as quickly as he would have liked. He worked hard to obey his father's dying request and booked the passage as soon as he was able to save enough funds to return home to marry, but it took him almost eight years.

While Ah Dang was too late to see his father alive, he made sure the man was not forgotten. His first act upon arriving in the hamlet of Longe Gonge Lay was to amass joss sticks and offerings of food and wine in front of his father's photograph at the household shrine. He burned long strips of red paper on which were written Ah Gay Sieng's name, so his father's spirit could join the ancestors. Ah Dang then visited his father's gravesite, where a bright-coloured marker identified the occupant, and repeated the offerings of a dutiful son to a revered and loved father.

Grave markers, 1986.
ROBERT WONG, CHINA

The cruellest aspect of footbinding was that ... peasant[s] ...
imitated the upper class. [A]mong Chinese farm women who
had to lead lives of work, footbinding ... was a widespread practice in the nineteenth century, and its effects were still visible in
the 1930s.

—John King Fairbank, *China: A New History*

FOUR

Grandmother's Golden Lilies

○

AH THLOO AND AH NGANGE: CHINA, 1923–1928

Of all the adult family members, Ah Thloo felt closest to her grandmother,
whom she called Ah Ngange. As the oldest person in the household, Ah
Ngange was recognized as the Elder. A wise and giving person, she held this
position graciously. She declined to be served first at mealtimes, choosing to
eat with the rest of the family. She could have lived a life of leisure, bossing
around her daughter-in-law, the servant girls, and the rest of the family, as
most women in her position did. She had earned the right, having lived in
a subservient position to her own mother-in-law in this very house, before
that venerable lady had passed on.

Her life had been especially difficult because she had *jat giek*, bound
feet, which made standing painful and walking excruciating. Before she
was married, she had rarely left her house, but as a young newlywed, she
had had to work in the vegetable gardens that her new family leased. Those
had been terrible, agonizing years.

Fortunately, when her son was born, her mother-in-law had allowed her
to stay in the house, even though he remained an only child. She was good at

managing the household servants and maintaining a harmonious home. In addition, she was good with her hands and an excellent cook.

Her dim sum, dumplings, were works of art. Every variety—whether it was sweet or savoury, steamed, boiled, or deep-fried—had a different wrapping or finish. Many of the wrappings required the creation of pouches to hold different fillings. No matter what the design, Ah Nange's finished pouches were uniform in size and shape, and their simple beauty made them even more appetizing.

She was also an expert seamstress; her handmade stitches were even and almost invisible. Her embroidery featured realistic-looking flowers, butterflies, and birds, all decorative without being gaudy.

When Ah Poy Lim, her son, brought his bride to the house, she had nurtured a warm relationship with the young woman, sharing the household duties. She maintained control of the house, while her daughter-in-law, whose feet were not bound, worked in the family's fields and gardens. Ah Ngange had specifically chosen for her son a bride whose feet had not been deformed.

Ah Ngange helped raise all the grandchildren once they were weaned from their mother's breast. Staying at home, she supervised their care, which was undertaken by servants (daughters of poor relatives). Everyone naturally doted on the first grandson.

When the granddaughters were born, Ah Ngange did not allow their feet to be tampered with. Although the practice was going out of favour, some families in the village reverted back to the tenth-century custom when they started to gather some wealth. Ah Ngange taught the girls the domestic arts. Ah Thloo learned the appropriate use of herbs, roots, and precious animal by-products for illness prevention, health, and healing. For example, mushrooms, because of their dark colour, nourish the kidneys. Similarly, green foods like vegetables benefit the liver, yellow soybeans help the spleen and stomach, red dates are good for the heart, and so on.

Ah Ngange treated the boys the same way as she treated the girls, but this was not customary. It was understandable that destitute families dreaded the birth of female children: girls were generally looked upon as belonging to another family—that of their future in-laws. As children, they had to be fed and clothed, and when they grew up, their parents had to provide dowries to marry them off. Granted, a bride price was paid, but when everyone was poor, how much could a family realistically get? Parents were never fully compensated for the care and attention a girl received at home, so it was little wonder that families sometimes took drastic measures. Occasionally, tiny, discarded corpses would be found, their small heads lying at odd angles to their perfect bodies, along the slopes of the rice paddy paths. Strangled and abandoned. All female. Dead male children were buried.

"Sons *are* important," Ah Ngange once said to Ah Thloo. "Unfortunately, no one remembers that *women* actually produce the sons."

When Ah Thloo was twelve years old, she was summoned to Ah Ngange's room one evening before bedtime. "Ah Nui, you are now old enough. Come, help your Ah Ngange wash her feet." By her tone, Ah Thloo knew that the term *Ah Nui*, meaning girl or daughter, was said with affection.

Ah Thloo did not hesitate, as she was honoured to help. "Ah Ngange," responded the girl. "What do you need?" She had always admired her grandmother's tiny feet; they were like a baby's, only daintier. Her own were square and blunt, ungainly in comparison. Also, she was secretly eager to see a *golden lily*, the term she had heard whispered by the village children. There was something exotic but also shameful in the term that she did not understand.

On the floor by her grandmother's wooden pallet bed, an enamel basin was filled with warm water and sweet-smelling herbs. In the corner of the room was a rough, three-legged stool that normally served as a chair. Ah Thloo was not invited to use it so she crouched on her haunches in front of Ah Ngange, who sat on the low bed. Her wide, bare feet were sturdy on the ground. This was a natural and comfortable resting position, and she could squat like this for long periods, with intermittent stretches.

With a grunt, her grandmother crossed one leg over the other and, hunching down, reached toward her foot to remove a tiny, embroidered, black cloth shoe. It was about three inches long, only slightly larger than a toddler's shoe. The foot was still encased in cloth. Ah Ngange found the end of the soft binding and started to unwind it carefully from around her foot. After a few turns, she stopped and handed the well-worn, yellowish bundle to Ah Thloo, indicating with a nod of her head that the girl should complete the task.

Pressing her lips together tightly in concentration, Ah Thloo took the roll from her grandmother and, as she had observed, held the unravelled end tautly in her small hands as she completed the task. When the last of the binding fell away to reveal the deformed limb, her body tensed and she felt tears of sorrow flowing like hot lava down her face, splashing down on what remained of her grandmother's foot. Still, she said nothing—no words could express her horror. This . . . this *thing* was as white as a lily, but it was like no flower Ah Thloo had ever seen.

Dangling from a pale, bony, atrophied calf was something that resembled a large white shrimp. The foot was bent, doubled over on itself, so that the front—where the toes should have been—was facing down, all the digits except the big one turned under. The toe-encrusted ball of the foot faced the flat of the heel, with only a narrow space between them. The big toe itself was stunted.

Looking at the broken foot, Ah Thloo realized that her grandmother walked, if her hobbling could be called that, on the base of her heels. Sighing audibly, Ah Ngange dropped the naked foot into the warm footbath.

"No need to cry, my girl," Ah Ngange said. "Grandmother's feet don't hurt now."

For once, Ah Thloo was reluctant to ask how and why, but Ah Ngange told her story quietly, as her weeping granddaughter continued to gently release the other foot from its bindings.

"I was four years old when my feet were first bound. Before that, I was free to walk, run, and jump, just like you. First, my feet were cleaned, the toenails cut, and then warm, wet cloths were wound around my feet. They were still small, but even so, the bindings chafed and I couldn't walk as before. My balance was all wrong. The first time my feet were released, I thought they were on fire. I was taught how to rub them and my legs to help the circulation. Just when I hoped the people had changed their minds, the bindings were put back on again. Each time, the wrappings were bound tighter. As my feet grew, they turned the four small toes under each foot. Whenever I walked, each step crushed the bones of my toes, but I never gave up trying."

She stopped speaking when the other foot was freed and submerged it eagerly.

"How horrible! It must have been so painful!" cried Ah Thloo, starting to get up to regain circulation in her haunches. Her grandmother laid a hand gently on her shoulder to restrain her.

"Yes, very painful. If you want to know how it felt at the beginning, try not to move at all, even when your legs start to hurt."

Ah Thloo lowered herself down and settled back to learn more, trying to ignore the tingling of pins and needles in her legs.

"I don't remember when the bindings started to force the front of my feet down to meet my heel. I learned how to care for them. Eventually, my feet *needed* the bindings to feel supported. The whole process must have taken about ten years. At least, that's when the pain started to dull. My feet stopped growing when I turned fifteen or so. In all that time, I don't remember ever sleeping through the night."

Hiccupping from her crying, Ah Thloo asked, "Ah Ngange, *hu-uck*, who did, *hu-uck*, this terrible thing to you?" She thought surely it must have been evil people who had forced such cruelty upon her beloved Ah Ngange. Hadn't she heard that bandits did unspeakable things to girls? "Didn't, *hu-uck*, your mother try, *hu-uck*, to stop them?" She was feeling shooting pains in her legs now and her back was throbbing, but she did not get up.

"It was my grandmother and my mother, of course."

Ah Thloo's eyes opened wide with disbelief, but she knew that her grandmother was telling the truth. "But it's so unfair!"

"Yes, unfair and unjust, because only girls suffer like this. It was tradition. Their own feet had been bound. Some traditions are good, some aren't. Unfortunately, we can't always tell the difference until it's too late. They believed this would help me find a good husband. I don't blame them. In one thing they were right—I was content with my life and marriage."

Then she whispered into her granddaughter's ear, "But I don't think the size of my feet made any difference! Times are changing and none of you girls will live with *this* tradition! When you're older, you'll understand that justice is worth fighting for. Get up now. Slowly . . . hold on to my hand. There you are." Her grandmother's strong hands gripped Ah Thloo's small ones. "How do you feel?"

"Thank you, Ah Ngange," murmured Ah Thloo, tears welling up again. "It feels like *ngai*, ants, are crawling up and down, pinching and biting!" Placing her weight on one foot, she cried out, "*Aiyahh*! How could you bear this for so long?"

"Wipe away those tears." Instead of answering, Ah Ngange reached over to massage Ah Thloo's legs and feet firmly. "This'll help you get back to normal. Do it this way. I need your help now. My bones are tired and I can't reach my toes. I'll show you what to do. My feet no longer like to be as free as a child's. We must work quickly to dry them, bind them up, and put them to bed."

Every night, until her grandmother died, Ah Thloo lovingly tended to the older woman's feet. While they were together, her grandmother talked about her own life, teaching Ah Thloo the womanly arts and much more. As she learned more about her grandmother, she learned about herself. Later, Ah Thloo would say, "Ah Ngange taught me how to survive, how to keep going. I learned that even people who love you will hurt you. She taught me about forgiveness. I am still learning."

o   o   o

AH THLOO: CHINA, 1925–1929

Girls were very rarely educated in the Guangdong countryside, but their move out of their family homes and into the nui oak was a type of finishing school. There, they learned about what the next part of their lives would be like, as wives and mothers.

The nui oak, similar to a bunkhouse, was mainly a place for the village's single girls to sleep at night. A building, perhaps an empty house left by a dead widow, was designated for this purpose. In large villages, each neighbourhood might have several such buildings, varying in size and capacity. It was traditional, in families with boys and girls, to separate them when they reached a certain age, usually when the girls started their menstrual periods. During the day, the girls returned home to perform their chores, work in the fields, and eat with their families.

They might be chaperoned by a local widow, who shared her knowledge, wisdom, and old wives' tales with the group; occasionally, an older, unmarried woman would move into the house permanently, to relieve the burden on her parents. An unmarried woman was a continuing encumbrance; at best, an embarrassment and at worst, a curse on the family. It was unlucky to include her as part of the family's ancestral tablets because it was believed that when an unmarried daughter died, she produced an inauspicious ghost. Women who had been abandoned by their husbands, or were widowed, might return to the nui oak to escape their in-laws, although this was rare.

At the nui oak, the girls had their own bed linens and kept their personal belongings in a semi-private space. But like girls everywhere and at any age, friends shared and borrowed things. They shared beds too; they had to, as there were never enough, not even in their own homes.

Their evenings and nights were spent in the company of females, and here they completed their education about womanhood. From traditional songs, they learned about the realities of marriage, how to cope with a difficult mother-in-law (all mothers-in-law were *expected* to be difficult), and how to be a "good wife": a good wife made sure her husband was fed, looked after his parents as if they were her own, produced sons, and worked hard. They memorized bridal laments and funeral dirges and learned how to mourn, thus enabling them to carry on two of the most important social customs in China.

While they sang, their hands kept busy, with embroidering, sewing, or weaving. They shared designs and techniques to make practical items for their dowries, such as slippers, quilts, or baskets. If they were lucky, they might sell their extras at the market town, earning some cash.

There were six to eight girls living in Ah Thloo's nui oak. One of her *day moy*, sister friends, was Ah Kange. They had different personalities: whereas Ah Thloo was quiet and contemplative, Ah Kange was boisterous; while Ah Thloo was diligent in her work, her friend loved to play. But they became inseparable.

Ah Kange's father was a rich merchant and landowner who often travelled to the cosmopolitan city of Guangzhou, and his contact with business people and foreigners exposed him to new ideas, one of which was to educate his daughter. However, he progressed prudently. Rather than send the girl to the village school where she would be in the company of boys, he hired a tutor to teach her reading, writing, and arithmetic at home, where his wife could chaperone. With enough servants to do the field and house work, Ah Kange went home each day to memorize written characters and learn arithmetic. She applied her knowledge of numbers to enhance her gambling winnings in games of chance during Gwoh Nien, the New Year festival, when itinerant peddlers, performers, jugglers, and hawkers set up business in the village.

Ah Kange brought a game of Mah Jong to the nui oak. Played with small oblong tiles, it has symbols depicting various suits (circles, bamboos, numbers, the four winds, flowers, and dragons). It is similar to the card game of gin rummy. Scoring is based on the combination of suits with winds, flowers, and dragons, and the winner is the first to collect a series of matching groupings using all her tiles. The game is played vigorously and quickly; the click-clacking and slapping of tiles adds to the excitement and fun. A quick eye and a good memory enhance strategy and the chances of winning.

Ah Kange loved to play, and her animated and good-natured vocalizations were infectious. When her time came to marry, she knew her parents would buy her trousseau items so she didn't need to make them. While some girls worked with their hands, she could always persuade three of them to spend their evenings playing with her. Most of the girls did not have cash to gamble with so they played with peanuts, an inexpensive and readily available snack.

Ah Thloo, although interested in watching the strategy from the sidelines, rarely played. Always frugal, she preferred to keep busy with her hands. Ah Kange, who won often, was generous with gifts of food or sewing supplies to Ah Thloo. At New Year's, Ah Kange insisted that Ah Thloo try her luck, and gave her cash with which to gamble. Ah Thloo found she actually enjoyed playing, but never got carried away and saved most of her winnings.

o   o   o

When Ah Thloo first moved into the one-room nui oak, the older girls were trading old wives' tales about men and women, and Ah Thloo heard more stories about "golden lilies." Getting ready for bed, they took turns washing their faces, hands, and feet in a communal basin on a corner stand. As each girl completed her cleaning routine, she emptied her dirty water into a collecting trough outside, so the next user could fill the bowl with fresh, cold water from a pitcher below the stand. There was a communal chamber pot on the floor behind a roughly woven cotton curtain. The contents of that pot were also emptied into the trough, and the mixture was collected each morning to fertilize the fields.

As usual, Ah Thloo was the last to come in, after helping Ah Ngange. Being a newcomer, she kept mostly to herself. She was often teased—it was the girls' way of getting the measure of a person. There were few secrets in a house of females. While some had grandmothers and mothers with bound feet, all the girls were unimpaired and none had seen an unbound foot. Ignorance made them variously curious, disgusted, and envious about Ah Thloo's secret knowledge.

"Well, the youngster has come in at last," said Pure Light. "I can smell her." At seventeen, the oldest girl in the nui oak, she was in danger of becoming an old maid. Her family, though fairly well off and anxious to have her wed, had yet to find her a willing husband. Unlike her name, she had a dark complexion with a personality to match. As the longest resident, she was the only girl who did not share a bed.

Ah Thloo still smelled of Ah Ngange's medicinal herbs. The allusion to her grandmother's bound feet was not lost on her, but she stayed quiet and commenced her own ablutions.

"I've heard that women with golden lilies do depraved things with men," taunted Pure Light. "I've heard that binding the feet produces muscles that normal, proper girls don't have—muscles that fuck!" The coarse word produced raucous laughter among most of the girls. Only Ah Kange remained solemn. She stayed seated but was poised to help her friend.

Ah Thloo couldn't ignore the remark; the spiteful words were dishonouring Ah Ngange. She hurled the bowl of water in which she had just cleaned her feet at the older girl, shouting, "Shut your ignorant mouth, you ugly old maid! If you, or anyone else, says anything disrespectful about my grandmother again, I'll pour the contents of the chamber pot on all your belongings," and she pointedly looked each girl in the eye. "And you'll never know when I'll do it." She braced her feet on the bare floor, preparing for a fight. Her face burned red, her eyes were hard slits, shooting daggers of defiance. She stared at Pure Light.

Pure Light sputtered and cringed from the cold, dirty water but didn't get up from her wet bed. For once she was speechless. No one laughed at her expense. A few of the girls stole furtive glances at one another, then at Ah Thloo. Their lips twitched at the corners, but no one spoke again that night. Ah Kange smiled at her friend.

o   o   o

In the nui oak, Ah Thloo also learned some radical and unusual ideas. One evening, Ah Kange held up a pamphlet that she had surreptitiously taken from under a pile of new books her tutor had brought. It was from the Kuomintang, a political party. The words *nui ngange*, female person, on the cover had caught her attention.

While Ah Kange read the dull, political contents out loud in an increasingly impatient and bored manner, Ah Thloo was astonished to hear such radically new concepts as equality between the sexes, a woman's right to inherit property, and protection for women who escaped from oppressive marriages. The pamphlet was probably a set of resolutions regarding women's rights put forward by the KMT Party's Central Women's Department. Written in formal language, the pamphlet's words were difficult for the girls to understand. Their lives up to that time had focused on hard physical labour just to survive; the concepts were confusing. What did "equality" mean? How could women "inherit" property when everyone knew everything belonged to the man's family?

They speculated about the meaning of "oppressive marriage." One of the girls reminded them of the night her mother had lost an eye. Her father had poked it out with his chopstick, blaming her for their poverty; he was enraged at having to eat watery rice and mung beans for six months. That night, and for some time afterwards, the girl had returned home to sleep with her mother.

Escaping bad marriages sounded like a good idea, but how would it actually work? Where would women go? How would they feed themselves and their children if they had no land to work, tools to use, or houses to live in? The girl's mother certainly had nowhere to go.

When the girl first told the story, Ah Thloo had been incredulous. Her own family members were civil toward one another and she had not been exposed to that type of cruelty. She wasn't sure how she would react if her future husband were to beat her. Working on the land had made her physically strong. Would she hit back? While Ah Thloo did not fully understand the concepts they gossiped about as teenagers in the nui oak, she never forgot them.

A woman's duty is not to control or take charge. Instead she must follow the "three submissions." When she is young, she must submit to her parents. After her marriage, she must submit to her husband. When she is widowed, she must submit to her son. These are the rules of propriety.

—Barbara N. Ramusak and Sharon Sievers,
Women in East Asia

FIVE

Maange Foon—*Blind Marriage*

○

AH THLOO: JANUARY 1929

"Father is back from the photographer's shop," Ah Thoo's mother said. "Hurry, pour him a cup of tea and make him comfortable while we look at the family portrait."

Ah Thloo had had her first photograph taken a few days before; her father was returning from the market town with a copy of it. She had just turned eighteen, and the photography session had created mixed emotions—it was exciting because it was a new experience but frightening because of its portents for her future.

What would she look like? Would the camera capture an image different from the one she had seen reflected in the dark mirror in her parents' bedroom? Not that she was vain—she had never had time to worry about how she looked to others—she was just curious. This likeness would last forever. She was glad the photograph had included her parents and her younger brother. Perhaps her father would give her a copy to keep after she was married.

The photographer had lent her some fancy clothes to wear for the sitting. The garments had made her feel *thloo muun*, sophisticated, even though they had smelled fusty, redolent of many other nervous, unwashed, adolescent female bodies. In the dressing room, she had posed before the small mirror, tucking each forearm into the opposite sleeve of her jacket, pretending to be a landlord's daughter with nothing better to do with her hands than hold a fan. She marvelled at the feel of her bare legs under the smooth fabric of the borrowed skirt. Her feet weren't quite as comfortable. For the first time in her life, they were encased in socks, which itched worse than leech bites, and stuffed into a pair of cloth shoes too small for her. She had been relieved to be rid of those encumbrances, and couldn't imagine anyone willingly wearing something so uncomfortable and impractical.

The feeling of those shoes cramping her toes gave Ah Thloo a sudden stab of grief for her beloved grandmother who had died only a short time earlier. She felt a simultaneous wave of empathy with her, as well as a renewed sense of pride in her grandmother's endurance. How she missed those private evenings by Ah Ngange's bedside!

The momentous photography session would start the next phase of her life. The photo was to be taken to the *Moi Ngange*, Matchmaker, who had found spouses for her three elder siblings. Ah Thloo's personal information would be noted and scrutinized by potential in-laws; that was the worst part.

Ah Thloo knew that at eighteen, she was getting to be a *law nui*, old maid, and as she grew older, it would be harder and more expensive for her parents to marry her off. After much deliberation, they had finally agreed that they should find a suitable husband for their last daughter. As it was, her marriage would stretch their meagre savings. It had been a difficult decision, reluctantly made, for Ah Thloo had proven her value to the family over and over again.

Ah Thloo had never complained, even though her young back was starting to curve from bending over in the rice fields. She had relinquished her responsibilities of caring for the family's water buffalo to her younger brother when she had moved to the nui oak four years ago, and besides working in the fields, she had also taken over the household chores from her ailing grandmother.

She was clever and creative with her hands. In the company of girls each evening, listening quietly to their gossip and singing the songs of life, Ah Thloo had been building up her trousseau and had completed a mosquito net, neatly embroidered bedding, and personal items like household slippers. Most of the pieces were created from carefully hoarded strips of used fabric. She had gratefully accepted skeins of colourful embroidery thread and beads from her friends for each Gwoh Nien, the New Year celebration.

Through her years of tutelage under Ah Ngange she had become a good cook. Her grandmother had taught her how to make a tasty meal in hard times out of whatever greens, grains, and tubers could be gathered. When times were better and they had meat, she could create a feast. For Gwoh Nien, she could wrap dim sum of any kind in uniform sizes. Everyone in the family agreed they were delicious, even when the stuffing was frugally short of meat. If mastery of the domestic arts was all that was necessary for being a good wife, Ah Thloo would excel.

"Of all our children, Ah Thloo has been the best worker," Ah Thloo had overheard her mother remark to her father. "I just don't know how I will manage without her."

"I know, but we can't afford to keep her at home much longer," Ah Poy Lim said. "In the last few years, with warlords and bandits roaming the country, everyone is afraid to build. *Aiya*, it has been so difficult!"

Ah Poy Lim had found it harder and harder to get paying work, but when Dr. Sun had taken back the reins of government in 1923, he was optimistic that increased unity would soon lead to peace and prosperity. However, Dr. Sun's untimely death and the subsequent riots in the cities in 1925 had added more uncertainty. Ah Poy Lim was not sure what he thought about General Jiang, the new leader of the Kuomintang Nationalist government. Now a civil war was being waged. He was thankful that the fighting was taking place far north of Guangdong, but the war was not helping the economy. Railways were destroyed and roads were blocked, preventing the safe passage of materials and goods to and from the countryside. Building materials became scarce and prices soared. The political events eventually took their toll on the local economy and on Ah Poy Lim's family; no one could afford to build houses. To help make ends meet, Ah Poy Lim worked the land, and whenever the battlefields shifted farther north and conditions in the south improved, he would return to construction.

For Ah Thloo, marriage became inevitable, and it meant marriage to a stranger. Few women looked forward to marriage—she was no exception. The concept of marriage for love was becoming fashionable in the big cities but was only a rumour in the countryside, where families still practised arranged marriages. What possible happiness could a woman gain from being shackled to a man whom she had never met and ordered about by his mother for the rest of her life? No wonder the girls called it *maange foon*, blind marriage.

However, there were no real alternatives. Ah Thloo was practical and obedient; she trusted her parents to find her a good husband. In addition, she was fond of children and wanted her own to love. She was a natural with them; all the neighbours' children wanted to be close to her.

But men—Ah Thloo had no understanding of them. She did not know how to communicate with them. Her closest relationships with men up to that time had been with her father and older brother. She supposed the relationship between her parents was optimal: they were always cordial to each other, and she never heard her father berate or beat her mother, even during bad times. When they were home, her brother and his wife appeared to have a similarly benign relationship.

While none of them had any interactions with boys or men, the girls in the nui oak still talked about sex. Anyone not blind would have seen the animals around them mating and giving birth, and those who had lived in small homes couldn't help but overhear intimate sounds between their parents in the night. Some of the girls had even helped their mothers during the birth of younger siblings, so they knew how and where babies came from. It all made for titillating conversations while the girls bent to their needlework, mending, and washing during the evening hours.

Now, Ah Thloo brought her father a small porcelain cup of fresh, hot tea, once he had settled in his straight-backed chair to review the new photograph. Resting on his lap was a large piece of folded brown paper. He had also invited his wife and younger son to join him in the *hiang*, common room. He sipped loudly on his tea, letting the air cool the scalding liquid to a drinkable temperature, while his family gathered and sat down. Ah Thloo served them too, before pouring herself a cup and sitting down beside her father.

With a practised hand used to rolling out architectural drawings, he

Left to right: Jiang Tew Thloo, mother Jiang Loo Shee,
father Jiang Poy Lim, younger brother Jiang Ngien Choo, 1929.
UNKNOWN PHOTOGRAPHY STUDIO, CHINA

delicately withdrew the photograph from the folder and with a flourish placed it on the table in front of his daughter. This was the most important record of her young life and it was going to determine her future. "See how beautiful you look!" he said with uncharacteristic emotion.

Recognizing his gesture of generosity and his affection for her, she looked up at him, saying simply, "Thank you, Ah Yea." Staring at her image, she thought with dismay: *I don't recognize myself at all! This girl looks so scared!*

o o o

AH DANG

"This one," said Ah Dang decisively, holding the photograph of a girl and her family. "Yes, this is the girl I want."

After an appropriate mourning period for his father, Ah Dang completed the selection process for his bride, and his marriage initiated another reinvention of himself.

Ah Dang was with his mother and the Moi Ngange, a woman well known in the market town. He and his mother had visited her a few days earlier and had negotiated and agreed on a price for her bride-seeking services. At their first meeting, she had asked him some questions about himself. They did not focus on his interests, hobbies, or personal preferences for a mate: those facets of his personality were superfluous, unworthy of a flea's consideration. The most significant information about him was his lineage and the specific date and time of his birth.

"I was born on October 11, 1902."

"Ah, you are a Water Tiger," the Moi Ngange said. "Those born under that birth sign are known for being sensitive, candid, and strong!"

"Quick tempered and obstinate too," Ah Dang's mother muttered under her breath, just loudly enough for him to hear. He pretended to ignore her barb, but his face started to colour.

As to the exact hour of his birth, he had to make up a time to give the Matchmaker. Not being superstitious, he didn't much care about its accuracy in defining his personality traits; he was a self-made man.

The next most important information the Moi Ngange required was his genealogy. He told her about his adoptive father's ancestors, never even considering his birth father's family line; it had not been relevant for a long time.

"Please accept my condolences on the passing of your illustrious husband," said the Moi Ngange, looking sincerely at Ah Tew May and then at Ah Dang. "And father." Of course the Moi Ngange had known of Ah Wong Gay Sieng's sterling reputation, his success in Gim San, his return to China, and his death eight years earlier.

Ah Dang saw her appraising look and guessed she was considering his worth. He looked modern and prosperous enough in his Western-style suit and leather shoes, and in fact, he *had* done well in Canada. He had stayed in British Columbia after landing in Vancouver in late 1921, and by the middle of the decade, the province was enjoying an economic boom. Roads were built to deliver services to remote communities. Provincial laws had forbidden the Chinese to work directly on projects involving Crown lands, but Ah Dang had used the new roads to cross the province and find work. Mostly, he cooked at various work camps during the summer and returned to Vancouver's Chinatown to work in restaurants, in whatever position he could get, in the winter. For a time, he lived in the pretty Kootenay town of Salmo. It was a supply centre for mining and logging and was the recreational hub for the region's workers. On his days off, he fished for wild salmon in the Columbia River.

He had few vices; remembering his birth father's gambling and opium smoking, Ah Dang was to forever shun those illusory, hope-draining habits. Instead, he saved most of his earnings. Like his adoptive father, he had decided to make Canada his country, but he intended to leave his mark in China too. In the meantime, he had lived a bachelor's life, free and unattached—until now.

He had to admit that he had felt the loneliness of being a young, vigorous, single man. He had watched as the old-timers took Aboriginal women as wives. The Indians, as they were called then, appeared to be more accepting of Chinese men than white society, even the women in the brothels. But not all white prostitutes could afford to turn business away. The comfort he bought from them was only physical and transient, and he wanted something more; perhaps a wife would fill the aching gap in his life.

Armed with the information he had given her, the Matchmaker had calculated his horoscope to help her select potential compatible candidates from her group of eligible girls. She dealt only with girls from respectable, merchant-class families in the district and selected a handful for Ah Dang's and his mother's consideration. For each candidate, she had a photograph and a written note, listing the girl's genealogy, vital statistics, and horoscope.

The Moi Ngange had only started telling them about the girls she had chosen and was about to launch into an enthusiastic endorsement of the third young woman in her file when Ah Dang made his comment. With the first two, the Moi Ngange had handed the photograph to his mother. She responded by making a discreet remark and handing the photo to her son. He would make the final decision.

Stealing another look at the third photograph in his hand, his mother murmured, "This one is a beautiful girl."

"She is more than beautiful. She has an inner beauty too. I can see her goodness. She is the one for me."

o o o

With the Moi Ngange as a go-between, the respective parents had agreed on the bride's dowry and the reciprocal *lai gim*, bride price. The dowry would include the items Ah Thloo had made as part of her trousseau. Her parents also bought the furnishings for the couple's bedchamber, including a woven bamboo bed with a headboard, a dressing table with a mirror and bench, a clothes cabinet, a wooden wash stand with a porcelain bowl and pitcher, and an intricately carved folding privacy screen. These would all be delivered to Ah Thloo's mother-in-law's house just prior to the wedding, ready for use on the wedding night. These items constituted her inheritance. As Ah Thloo would be moving to her husband's parents' home, it was expected that the furniture for the remainder of the house would already be there.

In addition, as a sign of betrothal, Ah Thloo's family would provide mounds of dim sum made by their village neighbours. There would be deep-fried *gai longe*—a crunchy pouch made from sticky rice flour with a savoury stuffing; delicately sweetened, steamed *fat gaw*—an egg-based cake; and chewy, steamed *choot tae*—a soft pouch made from sticky rice flour with a sugar filling. The dim sum were carefully layered between clean banana leaves, placed in woven baskets, and delivered to the groom's home by hired men travelling on foot.

The lai gim agreed to by Ah Dang included a large sum of cash; tins of fragrant teas; baskets of fresh fruits; an assortment of dried foods including mushrooms, shrimp, sea cucumber, and shark fins; several whole roasted pigs; and large baskets of live chickens, ducks, and geese. Some of the money would be used to buy gold jewellery, including thick necklaces, jade earrings, rings, and bracelets for the bride. All the gifts symbolized prosperity and fertility in different ways. His mother also bought stacks of special cakes, stuffed with lotus seeds and imprinted with the character for "double happiness," to be distributed to friends and relatives of both families to announce the couple's engagement.

The Moi Ngange had calculated that the earliest and most auspicious day for a match between Ah Dang and Ah Thloo was the eighteenth day of the twelfth month of the lunar calendar, so they had less than three months and the preparations were frantic.

Ah Thloo spent the two nights before her wedding day with her friends from the nui oak in her parents' house. During this time, called *nat gok*, the girls told stories they'd heard—or made up—about other people's wedding nights, and they practised some of the silly games the groom's relatives and friends were expected to play on Ah Thloo and her husband. The games had been initiated long ago as a way to frighten off evil spirits in the bridal chamber by making it noisy and crowded. The activities, such as making the couple peel and eat a single lychee fruit between them, with their hands tied behind their backs, were meant to make the partners interact physically and often involved opportunities to kiss and grope. For newlyweds, whose culture frowned on public displays of intimacy, the games were excruciating and humiliating. While both the bride and groom were targeted, the bride especially was expected to stay quiet and cooperative throughout.

Practising the games naturally led to talk about the wedding night. Traditionally, a piece of white cloth was placed on the bed and a bloody stain was displayed to the bride's in-laws on the following morning to prove she had been a virgin. A raucous discussion ensued when Ah Kange whispered conspiratorially, "In the city, no one bothers to do *that* anymore because the wedding couple gets so drunk, everyone stays virginal until the next night!"

The girls also sang songs lamenting the lot of women and the forced separation of a daughter from her family. The songs cursed the people who made this happen, including the Moi Ngange, the parents, and the future in-laws. Themes ranged from "My Parents Have Sold Me to Strangers Who Love [to Beat] Me" to "My Husband Is a [something uncomplimentary]." A favourite one was "My Mother Has a Black Heart":

> Radish white skin, black heart
> Skin is tight
> My mother has black heart
> Frightening black lips.

The girls shouted the words of this last song and wagged accusing fingers at Ah Thloo's mother, who pretended to cower in fright. Ah Shee herself had sung the same songs before her own wedding, so she did not take the accusations personally. In their perverse way, these activities were all part of a ritual for good luck in the coming marriage.

The songs were sung with gusto, accompanied by tears of sorrow. Ah Thloo would be sadly missed by her girlhood friends, and none of them knew if or when they would see her again. It all depended on whether her husband and in-laws would allow her to come home for visits, but then, some of the other girls would be married off too.

The girls laughed at the absurdity of arranged marriages, in defiance of their future mothers-in-law, and at the foolish behaviours of men. They took turns irreverently reciting ancient Confucian quotations about the characteristics of the "perfect woman." They reminisced, retold favourite stories about their times together, and laughed till they cried. Ah Thloo tucked away the memory of those two nights, to be opened and relived in precious segments during her future exile as a wife.

Before dawn on the day of the wedding, the girls helped Ah Thloo bathe and dress. As part of her wedding present, Ah Kange had given her friend a bar of sandalwood soap and had lent a tin bath from her home for this special occasion. Ah Ma had a neighbour draw clean water from the communal well, brought home in buckets carefully balanced on a bamboo carrying-pole, and poured into several large cauldrons to be heated over the coal fire. It took several trips to fill the container even halfway.

Squatting in the tub in her parents' bedroom, Ah Thloo had her first bath. She was helped by Ah Kange to be thoroughly scrubbed and massaged from scalp to toes; the rough cloth foamed with suds from the fragrant soap. The water had been infused with the skin of pomelos to ward off evil spirits. Brown ropes of *law nai*, old skin caked with dirt, floated in the water and formed a sticky ring around the tub. Ah Thloo's skin tingled from being newly exposed and the oils from the grapefruit rinds made her feel smooth and soft. Her long tresses were soaped until they squeaked.

"You have to smell beautiful for your husband—a Gim San law would expect it!" her friend said with a sly chuckle. She told the group of unbelieving girls that people in Gim San had tubs in which a whole body could be immersed in running hot water, and that the water was used only for bathing and nothing else!

Few people in rural China could afford to bathe: most just used a cold, damp cloth to wipe here and there. On occasion, they might immerse themselves, fully clothed, in the communal pond that served as a wash area for clothes as well as a watering hole for any of the village animals. The villagers might not emerge from the pond much cleaner, but perhaps they were a bit refreshed. All the water used on the wedding day would be skimmed, used to wash clothes, and finally to water the vegetable garden.

Ah Thloo was being very spoiled; even the rinse water was heated. Poured from a large, blackened kettle, the lukewarm liquid provided her with another new experience. Ah Kange almost dropped the kettle on her feet, doubling over in laughter at the way Ah Thloo sputtered and spat as the water streamed over her hair and face.

"Are you trying to drown me?" Ah Thloo shouted, finally joining in the laughter in spite of herself. "I'm not a cat!" For the rest of her life, she would never get used to holding her breath while water was poured on her head. She used the shower on her body but insisted on washing her hair by bending forward at the sink.

Rubbed dry after this pre-nuptial bath, Ah Thloo was ready to be dressed. Ah Ma had bought her a new red wedding outfit consisting of a full, floor-length skirt and a loose-fitting embroidered jacket. It had a traditional high collar, long, wide sleeves, and a side opening fastened with handmade frogs. Like everything else about this marriage, the outfit had not been chosen by Ah Thloo and she had not been asked for her opinion.

But it was the first piece of new clothing she had ever owned! If it had been made of the roughest cotton, and not silk, she would still have thought it beautiful. As each piece was put on, her calloused, work-worn hands caught on the smooth fabric but she couldn't stop touching it. She felt very sophisticated, just as she had at the photographer's studio. Her mother had also bought her a new pair of trousers and two new tops. The pieces would have to last for the three-day wedding celebration. Ah Thloo hugged her mother for the gift of clothes.

Of course it was Ah Kange who noticed. Everyone else was quite pleased with how beautiful Ah Thloo looked in the outfit, but she was missing a vital piece of clothing no one else had even thought about.

"What kind of panties will you be wearing under the skirt?" Ah Kange asked, after Ah Thloo's mother had left the room. No one wore bras—if one's breasts were large, one just bound them in place with a strip of cloth.

"What are panties? You know I only have two pairs of pants. I'm decently covered by this skirt . . . aren't I?"

"Panties are worn as *aie foo*, underwear. You wear them under your other clothes. The girls in the city wear underwear all the time," Ah Kange said knowingly. "As a bride you must have a pair, especially if you are marrying a Gim San law. He probably knows all about them!"

"But I can't ask Ah Ma to spend any more money! Where would they sell such stuff around here?" Ah Thloo was starting to panic, but her practicality soon took over. "It won't matter. By the time he finds I have no underwear, we will be married!"

"True, but wouldn't you like to show off how modern you are?" With a smile, Ah Kange presented Ah Thloo with a small, wrapped package.

Ah Thloo was speechless when she saw the silk bloomers. Ah Kange had to help her put them on, as the wedding outfit, with its long sleeves and skirt, made it difficult for her to manoeuvre; the smooth fabric kept slipping or getting caught up. Once on, the underwear, rubbing between her thighs, made her even more self-conscious.

Ah Kange also helped Ah Thloo make up her face with dabs of rouge on her cheeks and lips. The bride's hair was oiled, plaited, and wound into an elaborate bun on the back of her head. To complete the wedding outfit, a heavy, formal headdress, with a long fringe of red beads that covered her face, was carefully placed and pinned to her hair. The beads prevented her from seeing much of anything.

Fully dressed, she was finally presented to her parents. She kowtowed to them, bowing low to show her love and respect, and turned to bow several times in front of the family shrine. Then she bade them a final farewell as their daughter. When she returned for a visit, she would belong to another family.

Her friends started to cry again as they all made their way to the door of the house. From here, the bride was not allowed to *lok aye*, let her feet touch the ground. Ah Thloo was piggybacked from her house by a village woman and transferred to a *lieng giew*, a sedan chair, made of woven bamboo. A throng of relatives and village well-wishers crowded in front of the house and lined the streets. Preceded by professional announcers hired to let other villages know that a bride was on her way, and followed by transporters balancing her trousseau trunks and other bridal gifts on bamboo carrying-poles, Ah Thloo was borne to her future husband's village by a four-man sedan team. A long chain of tien, copper coins, tied together with red string, hung from the sedan. Its jingling length let onlookers know that this was a bride of some worth.

This was Ah Thloo's first long journey. Until then, she had walked everywhere, but she was being treated like an empress. That initial trip to her future home, less than twenty kilometres away, took most of the day on the meandering footpaths between the rice fields, particularly as the bridal column slowed down in each community to show off the trousseau. She should have been more afraid; she was alone, in the company of male strangers, going to an unknown destination. There was no possibility of distracting herself by gazing at the passing scenery because her headdress was firmly attached to her hair, and even if she had held apart the beaded veil, the sedan's heavy curtains would have obstructed her view.

She was going to marry "blind" in more ways than one. Not only could she not see the road ahead of her, she knew nothing about the man she was to marry. What did he look like? Would he like her? How should she act with him? The uncertainty made her heart pound like an exploding string of firecrackers at Gwoh Nien. All she had was faith—faith that her parents, who loved her, had tried their best to find her a good husband, faith that generations of women before her had survived blind marriages, and faith that her grandmother's wisdom, instilled in her being, would guide her to meet the challenges ahead.

Besides, it was too late to change her mind. Tied down and bolted securely on the outside, the doors of the wedding sedans were designed to prevent reluctant brides from escaping and making a run for it.

o   o   o

AH THLOO AND AH DANG: WEDDING DAY

Finally at her destination, Ah Thloo climbed onto the waiting back of another local village woman, to be piggybacked inside the house. There, the Moi Ngange greeted her and introduced her to Ah Dang by placing their hands together. Holding her, Ah Dang led her through the formal ceremonies that would make them husband and wife.

First Ah Dang guided Ah Thloo to the household shrine. Representing his ancestors was a photograph of his father and red ribbons with the names of his father's forefathers written in black ink. There, the couple kowtowed together before the display. Following a Western custom, he slipped a ring on the third finger of Ah Thloo's left hand. He also gave her a watch.

After the ancestor worship, Ah Dang led Ah Thloo to his mother. Again, the couple bowed low, showing their respect for her. The bride poured and formally served a cup of tea to Ah Tew May. By drinking the tea, she accepted Ah Thloo. She reciprocated by hanging the gold chains Ah Dang had bought around her new daughter-in-law's neck and slipping the solid, carved jade bracelets around her wrists. The couple was now formally married and Ah Dang parted the beads of the headdress to look at his bride's face.

Gazing up at him shyly but curiously, Ah Thloo saw for the first time the face of the man she had just married. He was very handsome, with intelligent-looking eyes and soft, full lips. He was smiling at her and his eyes shone brightly. He seemed pleased. His hands, holding the fringe open, shook a bit, and the beads jingled. He leaned into her face and gave it a quick, chaste kiss. He smiled again. This time she noticed a slight gap between his two front teeth.

Then he took her by the hand outside to the courtyard, where everyone had gathered to see the bride. The rest of the evening passed in a maelstrom of activity and noise as Ah Thloo was passed from neighbour to neighbour, to be gawked at, touched, and tested. The games began when the wedding banquet was served. Everything she did—the way she walked, how she held her chopsticks, what she ate, how she poured tea—was commented on. And everyone, except the bride, was allowed to share his or her opinion. At one point, Ah Thloo was helped out of her headdress, so the guests could have a better look at her face.

Throughout the festivities, Ah Dang was courteous and considerate. At the banquet, when traditionally the bride would eat with the women, apart from her new husband and the men, he had insisted on sitting beside her. Tea and rice wine accompanied the meal and Ah Dang had bought bottles of brandy for toasting. He picked out the best pieces from each dish with his chopsticks and placed them in her bowl. He kept her teacup filled. These were the tasks traditionally expected of a wife. He continued to hold her hand or pat her back. His constant touching made her blush and she had to remind herself that she was his wife and tried not to be startled or shrink from him. She supposed he had learned these odd manners living in Gim San.

After all the food and drink had been consumed and the wedding games played, the guests departed. All the furniture the bride had brought with her had been arranged in one corner of the small house, and the privacy screen had been placed at the foot of the bed. It would not be necessary for a while, as Ah Tew May and Ah Moydoy had moved into a neighbour's house when Ah Dang arrived. The couple was finally left alone.

He had not talked much during the evening, but that was all right—she had not known what to say to him either. His polite manners had made her feel more at ease, and by the end of the party, she felt she *could* talk with him. She was exhausted—physically, mentally, and emotionally. There was one more duty to perform, but from his previous behaviour, she thought he might be willing to consent to her suggestion to postpone conjugal relations to the next day. To her great disappointment, he reacted with rage.

"I've waited all these months for you! I will not be denied my marital rights!"

"I thought you had consideration. You don't care about me at all!"

"I chose you—you are mine. You *will* obey me!"

When she had refused to bend, he tried to break her with harsh words, accusing her of being un-virginal, insulting her. This infuriated her even more. In the end, he unhooked his leather belt and used it as a strap. When she fought back, he was so surprised that he stopped. He did not hit her again, but neither did he touch her until some days had passed. She later submitted—not to his will, but to her duty.

Their wedding night was not what either of them had expected. It resulted in humiliation and pain for both of them, and their misunderstanding, miscued actions, and angry words were to colour their relationship for the rest of their lives.

Another banquet was held the next afternoon, after their visit to the photographer's studio. Ah Thloo wore another of the new outfits her mother had bought and a few of the neighbouring women came to dress her hair. It was decorated with fresh flowers, in a style called *fa haang*.

Again, the neighbours ate every morsel brought out from the kitchen and drank to the last drop anything that smelled fermented until they had to resort to tea. On this occasion, Ah Thloo was allowed to speak. However, drained from the previous day's activities and *thlem tiek*, with a hurting heart, from the night's confrontation, she kept her opinions to herself. Everyone thought she was very virtuous.

One day after Ah Thloo and Ah Dang's wedding, 1929.
UNKNOWN PHOTOGRAPHER STUDIO

On the third day, her husband accompanied Ah Thloo back to her parents' home. There, they poured tea for her parents, and Ah Dang was acknowledged as their son-in-law. Following the tea ceremony, her parents presented Ah Thloo with their wedding gifts of gold and jade. There would never be much contact between her parents and her husband; thereafter, Ah Thloo would visit her parents on her own.

During the time Ah Dang stayed in China after the wedding, Ah Thloo used the legitimate excuse of working in the fields to avoid his company. She supposed that he had ways to keep himself occupied; she never saw him in the fields. She did not really care.

His words had hurt more than his physical abuse. Eventually, he apologized for forcing her and hitting her, but not for what he had said. When they were together now, he was gentle with her. But she could not forget his selfishness or his total disregard for her feelings in his barbed words, and her hurt prevented her from feeling any warmth toward him.

o o o

Ah Dang underwent another reinvention. Following the local custom, as a married man he was given another name. It was Libp Thlange, meaning "Establish Faith." While his mother stubbornly refused to change what she called him, his wife henceforth addressed him as Ah Libp Thlange.

He stayed in China for seven more months. He had seen something he liked in his bride on their wedding night. She had gumption and had fought back, kicking and scratching. He admired courage. He did not tell her about his feelings, but he was intrigued enough to stay with her, for a while.

It was an awkward period for both of them. Each was stubborn. Neither knew how to bend like the willow in the wind; each wanted to be the wind. During the day, they lived separate lives. He frequented the market towns and teahouses, trying to make sense of the rumours of a stock market crash and its subsequent effects around the world. With nothing invested, he hadn't been personally affected, but he was biding his time in China in the hopes that the economy in Canada would turn around.

He was also waiting for his wife to come to her senses. She finally did allow him his conjugal rights, but her attitude and behaviour toward him stayed cold. After half a year, he made plans to leave.

He made plans for her too. The Canadian borders were still closed to new Chinese immigrants, even to family members, so he could not take his wife with him. However, he had seen something else in her that would simplify their lives while he was in Canada. He had watched as she dealt with problems in the fields or with people in the hamlet. She worked things out. He saw her intelligence and was pleased that he had not married a "bamboo," someone who was empty-headed. He arranged for her to attend school to learn to read and write.

In the cities, integrated schools had been established for years, but the rural areas were still combating illiteracy in the general population. On farms, women were valued more for their labour than for their brains. Few families could afford to send their boys to be educated, let alone girls.

In every market town, professional letter writers would read the correspondence sent from foreign lands and compose the responses. Because of their education, they would also "interpret" the amount of money sent in a bank draft and "help" the recipient cash the cheque. The client had to trust in their honesty.

Ah Dang had worked too hard for his money to be cheated by dishonest letter writers, and Ah Thloo's education would prevent that from happening, but she would need every bit of gumption to stay in school; he knew his mother would not approve of his plan.

He told Ah Thloo what he had done for her in the way of schooling just before he departed for Guangzhou. She was then left behind to live with her mother-in-law and sister-in-law in their one-room house.

You are going to your home. You must be respectful. You must be careful. Do not disobey your husband. Thus to look upon compliance as the correct course is the rule for women.

—Hsia, *The Fair Sex in China*

SIX

Four Years, Four Months, Four Days

AH THLOO: CHINA, 1930–1934

During the years the couple was apart, Ah Thloo had a lot of time to relive their wedding night and the subsequent events. Had she married the right man? It was easy to dwell on the past, easy to stay hurt and rub old wounds until they were raw. It was hard to understand another person, especially when you didn't know anything about him. How do you build a life with a stranger who is living continents away? Still, she recognized that her life had changed, much for the better, because of her marriage.

What about their relationship; how had it happened? She had been afraid when she first met him. She knew only that he lived in Gim San and was older than she was by nine years. Then his hands lifted the heavy wedding veil from her face, and there he was! His smile was shy, but the warmth in his eyes suggested he was genuinely happy to meet her. But he was so different that first night—the memories from her wedding night still made her angry. She still could not refer to him by name without being reminded of that pain and disappointment. All she could hope for was that he would live up to the meaning of his new name, Libp Thlange, Establish Faith.

But what were her choices? Ah Thloo recalled conversations she had had with Ah Ngange a long time ago. They were initiated shortly after her third

67

elder sister had married but before Ah Thloo had moved into the nui oak.

"Ah Ngange, why do girls have to leave home after they get married? I don't want to leave you or the family. How will I be able to take care of you?"

"Ah Nui, you are my favourite foot bather! But someday you will want a family and a life of your own."

Ah Thloo knew she was Ah Ngange's *only* foot bather, but it had pleased her to hear the love in the old woman's voice.

"You must remember what I tell you, even if you don't understand it now. A woman's purpose is to create and nurture a *ga hieng*, a family and a home. This requires a special kind of *kien lake*, strength, to help her protect what she has created. It comes from deep within. It shows itself during times of greatest *foo*, bitter suffering. It can carry a woman through the loneliness of separation, mistreatment by a husband, the pain of childbirth, even the death of a loved one."

"But Ah Ngange, how would *I* build those strengths?"

"Ah Nui, you already have them!" her grandmother said. "In here, here, and here." Her work-hardened hands gently touched Ah Thloo's head, heart, and belly.

"How?"

With a hand on each side of Ah Thloo's head, Ah Ngange explained. "You are *liak*, intelligent. Some people, still too old-fashioned, say intelligence is not required in a girl. But don't you believe it! Girls have to be smart to survive. You are curious, you learn quickly, and you know how to apply your knowledge. All these qualities will help make your life better. Stay true to yourself—never deny your intelligence."

Moving her right hand to press Ah Thloo's chest, Ah Ngange continued, "You have shown courage and compassion. You know right from wrong. You help others in need. You have the courage to put your beliefs into motion and to protect the ones you love. From time to time, you may witness things, unjust acts that will anger you. But if you react with anger, you may choose the wrong path. Let your anger pass before you do anything. Always act from compassion and you will never go astray."

Finally, with her right hand on the girl's belly and her left hand directly behind, on her back, Ah Ngange made a prediction. In traditional Chinese medicine, this location on the body is a person's *thlem goyne*, heart-liver, meaning her core. "You have a great capacity for love. Your love will sustain you, give you greater courage in times of need, and will be returned a thousandfold."

At the time, Ah Thloo hadn't understood everything Ah Ngange said, but she had kept the words close to her, trusting in her grandmother's wisdom.

Shortly before Ah Dang left, he surprised her by insisting she learn to read and write. He had found a school in the neighbouring village of Nga Yieow and had paid the teacher to take her on as a student. He had also talked to his mother, who would get help in the fields so Ah Thloo would be free to attend classes and study.

At first, Ah Thloo was angry—he had done it again, arranged her life without consulting her! Then she remembered Ah Ngange's words and let her anger pass; it was clear that Ah Ngange was reaching out to guide her. She considered what he had just offered. An education. A chance to use the intelligence Ah Ngange had recognized. Perhaps this man valued intelligence in a woman. That attitude alone raised him up in her eyes more than anything he had said or done after that fateful night, and helped to mitigate the hurt. *Perhaps*, she dared to think, *he can see me as an equal.*

Going to school was a joy for Ah Thloo. It gave her something to look forward to, somewhere to get away to, because the atmosphere at home with her mother-in-law was hostile. The house they shared was a single, large, rectangular room, built in haste by her husband's venerated but long-departed father. The space was divided by pieces of furniture. Ah Thloo's marriage bed was in one corner behind the *thliew jiang*, folding privacy screen. It was further surrounded by the chest of drawers, dressing table, and washstand that had been part of her dowry.

Her mother-in-law slept behind her own bedroom furniture in the opposite corner with Ah Moydoy. A lazy girl, Ah Moydoy preferred to stay in and around the house and gossip with anyone who would listen rather than do her share of the work in the fields.

The cooking area occupied another corner. It was set up with the *daaw*, cooking hearth, a water reservoir, and a food preparation table, on top of which was a large wooden chopping board and cleaver. A small dining table, surrounded by four simple, wooden chairs, took up the remaining space, and constituted the communal living area.

When Ah Thloo did not immediately produce a grandchild, she felt the bite of her mother-in-law's disdain. The old woman and Ah Moydoy were like the two forks of a viper's tongue. Ah Thloo was treated like a slave, but school and her teacher were her salvation.

Ah Fonge Dange was the *thlange saang*, teacher, of the school in Nga Yieow. The village, about a twenty-minute walk from Longe Gonge Lay, was large enough to have a full-time, one-room schoolhouse, with permanent desks, chairs, and a blackboard. It wasn't unusual to have students of various ages at different levels of learning, but at nineteen, Ah Thloo stood out as a beginner.

Ah Fonge Dange taught the basics of reading, writing, and arithmetic. The students had to buy sets of books, one for each subject. In addition, they learned about the history of China. He kept the students informed of current events by teaching them how to read a newspaper. One day the teacher introduced the class to some writings by a man named Mao, who had been organizing unions in Hunan Province, on the northern border of Guangdong. Mao wrote about a "class struggle" between peasants and their oppressive landlords, who imposed heavy rents and taxes and high interest rates, and used exploitive labour practices, aided and abetted by corrupt officials. Ah Thloo thought back to her years with her fellow cowherds, recalling their abject poverty in comparison to the great wealth of people like the woman whose garden they had raided. What her teacher talked about in class opened her eyes to the world beyond the boundaries of the market towns.

The students learned to read and write the same way they learned arithmetic, by rote. Each day the teacher selected a passage from a book and read it through while the students followed the text with their fingers. At home that night, they would *niem see*, memorize the text, and prepare to *mak see*, write the piece from memory, the next day. They also had to be ready to be called on to stand up for an oral recitation.

Applying her mind to the task of learning was a challenge Ah Thloo loved. It took all her concentration to keep up with the class. She already knew she had a good head for numbers, and she soon caught up in the other subjects with children who had been in school for many more years.

In 1931, the teacher had much tragic news to report. That summer, the Yangtze River flooded, killing more than one hundred and forty-five thousand people, while fourteen million refugees were left stranded. In the fall, the Japanese invaded Manchuria, which threatened the sovereignty of

China. In 1933, the name of Mao again came up in discussion, this time associated with the Chinese Communist Party, which was being attacked by the government.

At home, when Ah Thloo was nagged by her mother-in-law, or confronted by her sister-in-law, she would recall something new she had learned that day and mull it over. Hard labour and trivial tasks could be endured when her mind was occupied elsewhere, and eventually she devised a plan to buffer herself even more securely.

Ah Thloo's new home, the *nonge toon*, rural hamlet, of Longe Gonge Lay, an offshoot of the much larger village of Cha Liang about a ten-minute walk away, had been built by a group of brothers named Wong. A number had made their money working in Montreal, Canada. The second brother, Wong Oy Lan, known as Ah Ngay Gonge, or Second Elder Uncle, had invited his distant relative, Wong Gay Sieng, Ah Dang's adoptive father, to build there as well, when his family abandoned their ancestral house and village after being targeted by bandits. Unfortunately for his wife, on that trip Ah Gay Sieng stayed in China only long enough to build a small house for her and their son. When he returned home for the last time, he was too sick from cancer to even initiate an expansion of their house before he died.

The hamlet consisted of nine houses, built in pairs, lined up in five rows. Between each row and each two-house block was a lane; each house had a front and back door leading out to the main lanes. Across the lane from one door of Ah Tew May's house was where Ah Ngay Gonge's wife and two of his three daughters lived. His eldest daughter, Ah Ngan, had married even before her youngest sister was born and lived in a village an hour's walk away. She was the same age as Ah Thloo, and they came to know each other later, when Ah Ngan came back to her family's home during Kong Jien, the War of Resistance against the Japanese.

The middle daughter, Ah Lien, became Ah Thloo's best friend in the hamlet during this time and they attended school together. The youngest daughter, Ah Aie, was not even two years old when Ah Thloo moved to the hamlet, but she soon became one of the "girls." The families produced many boys, all cousins to Ah Lien and Ah Aie, but the hamlet was too small to have a nui oak. Ah Thloo helped the village and herself by inviting the sisters to study and sleep with her, creating a nui oak. At school she was a star student; the girls looked to her for help and they enjoyed each other's company. They also provided a buffer between Ah Thloo and her spiteful relatives.

Meanwhile, she put her new knowledge to effective use. Ah Dang wrote regularly and always enclosed a money order. She was proud of being able to correspond with him and to manage their financial affairs on her own at the bank in the market town. While he could not always send much money, she was grateful for his financial support. She was very aware of the women around her who lived in poverty, neglected and abandoned by their husbands who were abroad. As the years went by, she started to feel more comfortable about her own husband and their marriage.

o   o   o

AH DANG: MONTREAL, 1930–1934

When Ah Dang returned to Vancouver on July 14, 1930, he continued to use the immigration receipt under the name of Wong Guey Dang. Some things were not worth changing.

But the city *was* very different; the Depression had hit hard in British Columbia. Its economy was so dependent on natural resources that when commodity prices for lumber and minerals plummeted, the suffering was widespread.

Layoffs had begun in Vancouver sawmills in 1929, and government agencies responded only reluctantly to Chinese requests for aid. Traditional self-help agencies in Vancouver's Chinatown, such as the Chinese Consolidated Benevolent Association (CCBA), could not meet the demand from the growing numbers of unemployed Chinese. Local Chinese restaurants supplied meals to the needy. By 1931, 80 per cent of Chinatown residents were idle. Some resorted to begging. It was cheaper to buy them passage back to China than to support them, and as the Depression progressed, the BC government paid for a few hundred men to return to China, stipulating they not come back to Canada for a minimum of two years.

Not long after Ah Dang's return to Vancouver from China, he received a life-changing letter from Ah Ngay Gonge, who owned a laundry business in Eastern Canada. Ah Dang had maintained contact with him and looked up to him as a surrogate father after Ah Gay Sieng went back to China and died. Now, Ah Ngay Gonge became Ah Dang's benefactor too. He invited Ah Dang to join him in Montreal because, while the city had not escaped the Depression, more job opportunities existed for Hong Ngange, Chinese people, there.

Ah Dang was ready for a change and this was probably a prudent move. As it was, Ah Ngay Gonge had not left him much choice in the matter; in his letter, he had included a one-way train ticket on the Canadian Pacific Railway from Vancouver to Montreal.

The train left Vancouver in the evening. Unfortunately, it went through the Rocky Mountains in the dark of night. The closest Ah Dang had been to that area was when he had worked in the southeastern BC town of Salmo. He had only heard about the vast mountain range, with peaks so high they never lost their hats of ice and snow, and was disappointed that he would not be able to see them on this journey. Peering out into the growing darkness, he could perceive little outside the window of his bunk. Although the rhythmic click-clacking of the tracks and the undulating motion was making him tired, he felt the need for one last pee.

Balancing his way along the swaying car in the dimly lit hallway toward the washroom, he accidentally bumped into a Chinese porter.

"Pardon me," Ah Dang said in Chinese. "I was looking down and didn't see you coming."

"No, sir, it was my all fault," responded the porter in a similar dialect. "I apologize for my clumsiness."

"What's your family name?" Ah Dang asked.

"My name is Li. I am from Toisan," replied the porter, understanding that the man had wanted to know where his family was from in China.

"Eh, what? My family name is Wong, from Hoyping. Ah Bak, Elder Sir, we're neighbours!" Ah Dang guessed the man was older than his own twenty-nine years.

Ah Dang asked Ah Bak about the Rocky Mountains and his job on the train. Just as their discussion led them to talking about their countrymen who had built the railroad, the train whistle blew.

"Craigellachie. This is where the last spike was hammered in, in 1885," said Ah Bak. "Did you know, not a single Chinese was invited to attend the ceremony?"

"We Chinese have had bitter lives, eh? I heard that the CCBA collected the bones of more than three hundred corpses and returned them to China for decent burial."

When Ah Dang got back to his bunk later that evening, he found he couldn't sleep. There were too many ghosts of his countrymen, whose mortal bones were still waiting to be found and buried properly, wandering the mountains.

o   o   o

Ah Ngay Gonge welcomed Ah Dang at Montreal's impressive Windsor Station and offered him a place to stay. His home and laundry business were on St. Hubert Street, not far from the train station. They took the number 150 bus east on Dorchester Boulevard.

To help repay the cost of the train ticket, which Ah Dang insisted on doing, he helped Ah Ngay Gonge with the laundry. He scrubbed the garments on a wood-and-glass washboard until his hands and knuckles were raw from the harsh laundry soap. He learned to mend, starch, iron, fold, stack, wrap, and mark the finished items for each customer. The laundry consisted mostly of men's white shirts, underwear, and socks. Sometimes, if he was home during the day, he helped out at the counter. During the day he looked for work, mostly in restaurants, but few people were hiring.

Wages for jobs that still existed were low. A full-time electrical technician at the prestigious Marconi Company was paid fourteen dollars a week, while a waitress might work for a few hours a day at forty-five cents per hour. A full meal, consisting of a bowl of soup, two slices of bread with butter, a main course of fish or meat, a spoonful of mashed potato, dessert, and coffee, cost only twenty-five cents, but few people could afford to pay even that amount. Rent for a room was seven dollars a week; a house might rent for twelve dollars a month. Without work and wages, however, many were forced to live rough on the streets or squat in abandoned or condemned buildings. Ah Dang was lucky to be living with Ah Ngay Gonge.

Ah Dang often walked by a large church on Bleury Street that had a noontime soup kitchen. Passing the open door, he saw that the kitchen provided a bowl of soup and two pieces of bread. He had expected to see adults but was shocked to see so many children in the lineup, some clinging listlessly to their mother's filthy skirts, others sprawling limply on the ground, too hungry and tired to cry. He was reminded of his long-forgotten childhood, before he was reclaimed. His heart ached for the children, but there was nothing he could do to help them.

One of Ah Ngay Gonge's regular customers noticed Ah Dang's English. Although he spoke with a strong accent, he was quite fluent. Over the next few weeks, they exchanged a few pleasantries and Ah Dang mentioned his previous work experience; the customer offered him a job as his family's cook.

Ah Dang was thus reinvented as a domestic servant for a wealthy white family (whose identity is now unknown) who had managed to survive the stock market crash. All his years of cooking in camps throughout BC were finally paying off. After passing a trial period, he was offered a modest monthly wage, most of which he literally socked away, as well as room and board. He stayed with the family until late 1934.

His guide was *The Boston Cooking School Cook Book*, by Fannie Merritt Farmer, published by McClelland & Stewart. He wrote his name, Wong Guey Dang, in neat script on the inside page, and he bookmarked pages with small, accordioned booklets of cake recipes distributed by Swans Down Cake Flour. He also collected recipes from the newspaper, written on scrap paper. One of these was a recipe for almond bars. Another was a cocktail recipe, calling for limes, rum, and egg whites.

On his days off, he went sightseeing in the city. When he first arrived in Montreal, Ah Ngay Gonge had taken him to Chinatown, which was then clustered along De La Gauchetière Street West, between St. Laurent and Jeanne Mance, and Dorchester Boulevard and De Vitre. There, Ah Dang was introduced to the major Chinese organizations.

As a hand laundry operator, Ah Ngay Gonge was very involved in the Chinese Association of Montreal, an organization similar to Vancouver's CCBA. One of its activities was to defend operators' rights and fight the mounting fees imposed by the provincial government. In Quebec, hand laundries were by far the single largest occupation of the Chinese. They worked long hours, for low returns, and were seen as competing against white women who took in laundry. In 1915, a licence cost fifty dollars, but Chinese operators were charged an extra fifty. In 1932, the association held off a proposed hike of one hundred dollars by the municipal government.

Ah Dang joined the Wong Wun Sun society, a clan association; it was a place for members to socialize and exchange news about China and their families. The stories from China brought mixed reactions. On the positive side, the Kuomintang Nationalist government was trying to bring order out of the chaos that had marked the warlord period. Ministries were created to deal with international affairs, such as war and regaining Chinese sovereignty in foreign relations, as well as with domestic issues of finance, education, and justice. But in 1931, Japan invaded Manchuria and established the puppet government of Manchukuo. A year later, the Japanese established a military presence in Shanghai, and while the incident did not lead to war, the Japanese made their way into northern China through demands and negotiations. However, instead of repelling the foreign invaders, General Jiang spent his resources fighting the Chinese Communists, raising great indignation among students and intellectual activists within China and elsewhere.

With growing frustration, Ah Dang watched the advance of the Japanese by reading Chinese newspapers. While Ah Thloo, his mother, and her adopted daughter were relatively safe in the south of China, he felt it would be only a matter of time before the determined Japanese forces overtook the whole country, if Jiang continued to ignore the foreign threat while fighting his personal civil war.

As a diversion from the news of China, Ah Dang looked into activities offered by the churches serving the Chinese population of Montreal. The Chinese Catholic Mission had existed since 1918; its greatest contribution was the mission hospital, run by the Sisters of the Immaculate Conception and funded by the Chinese community. Initially established to deal with the worldwide influenza epidemic, the mission bought a building on Lagauchetière Street West two years later, to serve as a hospital for chronically ill, single men with no relatives. The mission sisters and doctors volunteered their services. There was also an outpatient dispensary, where Chinese from as far away as Halifax came for treatment. Ah Dang would later donate funds to help build a new hospital on St. Denis Street, away from Chinatown.

The Chinese Presbyterian Mission was started in 1897 by Chan Nam-sing and Joseph Thompson, missionaries from China. Whereas Catholics were more apt to follow dogma, dismissing all ancient Chinese traditions, Pastor Chan was more flexible. He did not pressure the Chinese to abandon ancestor worship, and interestingly, he and his family followed the Chinese lunar calendar and celebrated Chinese New Year; when his son, Paul, was born, they celebrated the child's one-month birthday by giving out dyed red eggs. He also allowed non-Christian Chinese to be buried in Mount Royal Cemetery. The Presbyterian Church offered Canadian-born Chinese a kindergarten, a band, a Canadian Girls in Training group, a Chinese school, and a young people's society.

Montreal started to recover from the Depression in the mid-1930s. Ah Dang watched with fascination the construction projects of the day, including the Jacques Cartier Bridge linking Montreal with Longueuil on the south shore and the Sun Life Assurance Company building on Dominion Square. When it was completed in 1933, it was the tallest building in the Commonwealth. During the Second World War, the Bank of England stored five billion dollars, including gold bullion, there, and the vaults were rumoured to have held the British Crown Jewels. Little did Ah Dang know then that he would own property across the square from the Sun Life building.

In 1932, the city passed a resolution to establish the botanical gardens, which became one of the best-known botanical gardens in the world. It was one of Ah Dang's favourite places to visit. He also enjoyed spending quiet afternoons sitting by the pond at La Fontaine Park, reading a newspaper or feeding the ducks.

After 1891, when the major department stores moved from the business district of Old Montreal to St. Catherine Street, between Bleury and de la Montagne, that location became the bustling centre for shopping, with Henry Morgan's, Eaton's, Simpson's, and Ogilvy's. Of these, Ah Dang considered Ogilvy's the most prestigious, its products the most exclusive. If he could shop there, he would know he had made it. However, he was disappointed to find that as he strolled through their menswear department one day, the sales clerks refused to serve him. It may have been because of his race—he never found out why.

A few years later, he returned to Ogilvy's, walked deliberately to the men's fine clothing section, and bought a cashmere sweater. With cash. Just to show them he could.

o   o   o

AH THLOO AND AH DANG: CHINA, 1934–1935

In October 1934, Mao Zedong and Zhou Enlai led the Communist Red Army troops on a ten-thousand-kilometre trek from Jiangxi Province in the south to create a stronghold in Shaanxi in the north. They were fleeing Kuomintang attacks. One hundred thousand people started the trek but only four thousand completed it. Known as the Long March, the dangerous journey, which ended in October 1936, built the reputations of Mao Zedong, Zhou Enlai, and Deng Xiaoping, as well as many of the country's subsequent leaders.

In the same month in 1934, Ah Dang left Canada for China to visit his family. He had saved his money and it was time to show off his wealth by expanding the house for his mother and his wife. His intention was to add on to the existing, single-room structure by building around and up. He would ask his father-in-law, Ah Poy Lim, to help. With his building skills and local knowledge, the older man could draw up the plans, find appropriately skilled labourers, and obtain the finest materials, all at the best prices.

Ah Dang arrived in the hamlet exactly four years, four months, and four days after he had left. The word for four, *thlay*, is a bad word in Chinese—it sounds like *thlay*, the word for dead. For Ah Thloo, November 5, 1934, felt a bit like death, for on that day, she lost her freedom.

When Ah Dang arrived, he immediately changed the living arrangements. At least, he tried to. While it was relatively easy to move Ah Tew May and Ah Moydoy across the lane, into his benefactor's house, he did not have the same level of cooperation from his wife. He never asked why the two neighbour girls were sharing his marriage bed with Ah Thloo; he just acted.

As before, Ah Dang used the strap. Again, Ah Thloo fought back, and this time, she lashed back with her tongue as well. Living in the house with Ah Tew May and Ah Moydoy had taught her how to hurt with words. She had buried away all the snide remarks they had made about him over the years, all the secrets about him as a boy, and she dredged them up to use against him. As before, he was stopped short by her ferocity—and now by her words.

After that, Ah Thloo was even more adamant that the girls stay with her; she needed them to protect her from her husband. He gave up, temporarily. He had other things to attend to and soon forgot the incident.

Ah Dang asked his father-in-law to quickly build a small, temporary shelter for himself and Ah Thloo while work continued on the main house. He also agreed to have his elder brother-in-law, the artist Ah Gim Yoke, decorate the house with tiles and paintings. The two got along well, and Ah Dang was glad to help improve his brother-in-law's precarious financial situation. Their congenial relationship led them to have a photograph taken together.

Ah Dang (on the right) and artistic brother-in-law Ah Gim Yoke, 1935.
UNKNOWN PHOTOGRAPHER STUDIO, CHINA

Ah Dang's house is the closest one on the right side of the lane, 1986.
ROBERT WONG, CHINA

Kitchen hearth, 1986.
ROBERT WONG, CHINA

Neighbours share a meal in the main room. Ah Lai is second on the right, writing, 1986.
ROBERT WONG, CHINA

Household shrine, 1986.
ROBERT WONG, CHINA

One of the bedrooms, 1986.
ROBERT WONG, CHINA

Building materials and labour were cheap. The Depression had reached China, especially in the manufacturing sector; in Shanghai alone, more than one million people were out of work. In the countryside, if cash was not available, one could at least work for a bowl of rice at the end of the day. Labour cost only half a yuan (seventeen cents) per day per person. A three hundred-pound bag of cement was less than one and a half yuan (fifty cents). Ten thousand bricks could be bought for only one hundred yuan (thirty dollars). Ah Dang's father-in-law oversaw the building and kept a meticulous list of materials in a string-bound, rice-paper booklet.

The small house was completed in a matter of days, and somehow, Ah Dang was able to coax Ah Thloo into living there with him. There was no room for the sisters; they had to return to their own home.

Ah Thloo was relieved to live apart from Ah Tew May, the devil she knew, but it was like jumping from the wok into the fire, to live with this strange, volatile man by herself. Still, he was calmer now and was solicitous with her. Once more, duty called and she complied. They maintained a relatively harmonious household, and the goddess Kuan Yin, "One Who Sees and Hears the Cry from the Human World," blessed them with a peace offering: Ah Thloo became pregnant. When Ah Dang learned of this, he made sure she had the best medical care money could buy from the surrounding market towns. He asked his mother to cook nourishing broths, and the pregnancy proceeded with ease.

The main house was built in record time; it was large, more spacious than any other house Ah Dang would ever live in. It was deliberately plain from the outside, with grey brick walls and thick, iron-reinforced wooden doors. All the windows on the first floor of the two-storey building were secured with vertical iron bars, and the house was attached on one side to its neighbour. All this was done to discourage bandits and other invaders.

The ground floor was divided into three sections. The front door opened into the first section, which had two rooms. One was a cooking area. The other was a storage room, with two windows to let in light and air. In the corner by the door, a bamboo ladder climbed upstairs.

From the kitchen, a doorway led into the original *hiang aie*, main room. A large opening, cut in the ceiling, made this room bright and gave it a feeling of airiness. Upstairs, a banister with green dowelling and a red railing surrounded the opening. Emerald-green and white decorative tiles, designed by Ah Gim Yoke, lined the balcony and the rest of the ceiling. He also created large paintings, of birds and scenery, on the walls above eye level in the downstairs room.

At one end of the room, on the other side of the wall from the kitchen, was a reservoir. Water, drawn from the communal well and carried by wooden buckets suspended at either end of a bamboo pole, was stored here. A dining table stood next to it and a staircase at one end of the room led to the second floor.

Not only people used this room—chickens, geese, pigs, and even calves lived there as well. It was not the most sanitary arrangement, but when bandits roamed the area, inside the house was the safest place for the animals. On the other side of the hiang aie was the third section, again divided into two rooms, used mainly for storage.

There were four rooms on the second floor—two on either side of the landing. Ah Dang and Ah Thloo had a room on one side of the balcony while Ah Tew May and Ah Moydoy slept in a room on the other side. The other two rooms were for storage, where large ceramic urns kept rice and other foodstuffs dry and safely away from hungry rodents and insects. The upstairs rooms were particularly handy during the flood season, when the ground floor could fill with brackish water partway up the stairs. A portable coal-burning stove served as the cooker whenever the family had to live upstairs. To the left of the stairs stood the indoor ancestral shrine and at the far end of the house, facing the communal bamboo garden, was an open deck, part of which was enclosed as a lookout area and safe room.

No bathrooms were built into the house, as no infrastructure existed in the small hamlet for plumbing, for either incoming water or outgoing waste. The hamlet's well did not provide enough water to allow for baths; those people who did wash made do with sponge baths, using a small basin. The communal toilet was at one end of the hamlet, under a shelter built of woven bamboo. It consisted of a very large ceramic pot, standing about four feet high, accessed by brick steps. Night soil was still the main source of fertilizer.

Ah Dang and Ah Thloo had a few months to move in all the furniture, which had been stored in various neighbouring houses, before their first child was born. Although the midwife had an excellent reputation, when she came to help Ah Thloo deliver the baby, Ah Dang insisted she wash her hands with soap he had brought from Canada and in hot water that had been boiled. He also insisted that the sheets and blankets for the birth and baby swaddling be washed with hot, soapy water. He had learned the importance of hygiene in the home of his white employers in Montreal.

The first child was born on the twenty-eighth day of the eighth month of the lunar calendar, in 1935. Ah Thloo, thinking her husband might be disappointed with a female, was ready to defend the child's life with her own, but she was pleasantly surprised to learn that he had been concerned only for the health of the baby, not its sex. Whenever he held the infant, his face lit up with delight. He smiled broadly and his eyes sparkled. *Another piece of the puzzle that makes up this man, the father of our daughter*, Ah Thloo thought.

Ah Tew May was also transformed by the baby. At first, she derided Ah Thloo for giving birth to a mere girl, but Ah Thloo reminded the older woman of her *own* children. Also, children have a way of melting even the hardest of jade-cold hearts. After so many years, here was a baby to care for, to amuse, and to entertain. Ah Tew May seemed to forget herself; her tongue lost its sharpness. The words she spoke to the baby were sweet, and she carried on in the same tone when she was speaking to Ah Thloo. With the baby, her attitude was one of tenderness. With her daughter-in-law, Ah Tew May was now solicitous, always offering to help whenever the baby needed cleaning or wanted to be picked up. However, with her adoptive son, she still struggled to bite her tongue. Now and again, Ah Dang and Ah Thloo thought they saw Ah Tew May's mouth twitch upwards at the corners, especially when she was engaged with the baby.

During the baby's *gat how*, the one-month ceremony, she was named Lai Quen, "Most Beautiful." After the child underwent the traditional hair-cutting ceremony, she was officially presented to the world to receive gifts. With the completion of his house and the start of his family, Ah Dang could have made plans to leave, but he stayed two more months after the celebration.

Although he had been away from Canada for only thirteen months, as if to hurry his return he was surrounded by bad omens. Both the Yangtze and Yellow rivers flooded, while in thirteen other provinces in China, droughts caused devastating crop failures. Ah Dang worried about the dreaded possibility of the Japanese arriving in the south. The Communist Red Army was still making its way north. If actual war broke out, he could be stuck in the country, of no use to his family. At least if he was in Canada, he could work and send remittances.

He had not bought any land. Ah Thloo leased a plot of land to grow vegetables and she had used his remittances carefully to purchase rice, as well as some chickens and pigs to raise for market. She was always able to negotiate a price that included a large chunk of fresh meat to bring home, so the family had not gone hungry over the past few years. He was proud of her.

Before departing, he entrusted Ah Thloo with the remainder of his funds, hoping it was enough to outlast whatever happened, until he could send more money. Cursing the Chinese generals and Japanese invaders for endangering the lives of his family, and the Canadian government for keeping him apart from them, he made a reluctant departure.

This time, their separation was even longer.

A woman's duties are to cook the five grains, heat the wine, look after her parents-in-laws, make clothes and that is all!
—Liu Hsiang, *Biographies of Admirable Women*

SEVEN

Abandoned Heroine

AH LAI: CHINA, 1945

When Ah Lai, Ah Thloo's daughter, was ten, the War of Resistance Against Japan, or Kong Jien as it was called in Chinese, had been raging for eight long years, bringing terror and deprivation. Her mother had run out of money and had no way to earn it. The fields had been planted, but when the harvest was still twenty days away, the whole hamlet was dangerously short of food. Ah Lai was to plead with Ah Hoo, Mother's Mother, for a loan of *mai*, raw rice, to tide them over, just till the harvest. It was a great risk—Ah Hoo had turned them away before, when they had offered their labour; now, they had nothing to give in exchange. Standing outside the door, Ah Thloo urged Ah Lai forward into her former family home.

It was a big responsibility, and the little girl trembled as she was pushed inside, but as soon as she looked around the house and saw the walls lined up to the rafters with bags of rice, she felt a flood of relief. *They have so much; why wouldn't they share? Of course I will be successful with my mission!* so Ah Lai thought.

o o o

AH THLOO AND AH LAI: CHINA, 1936–1945

The women were once again left on their own to defend themselves in China.

A view from the lookout balcony, 1986.
ROBERT WONG, CHINA

A year after Ah Dang returned to Canada, General Jiang of the Kuomintang (KMT) Nationalist government negotiated a ceasefire with Zhou Enlai in the civil war with the Chinese Communists. This was just in time because seven months later the Japanese invaded China. When Nanjing fell to the Japanese, the government relocated its capital to Chongqing. The Communists were headquartered in Yenan. For a time, from these separate bases, the two factions came together in a formal, if fragile, united front to strategize and fight their common enemy.

Guangzhou was occupied by 1938, but the Japanese forces stayed mostly in the city. However, they made occasional forays into the countryside, and whenever that happened, the human alarm system alerted everyone in the fields.

"*Ngake Voin-doy*, the Japanese are coming!"

Ah Lai, at the age of three, was taught to run home quietly or hide in caverns dug into the hillocks and designed to be inconspicuous. Everyone in the surrounding area had heard about the atrocities perpetrated by the Japanese, especially during the Rape of Nanjing in 1938, when three hundred thousand men, women, and children were massacred. Stories abounded about live babies being ripped out of their mothers' bellies and skewered onto Japanese bayonets, children taken as sex slaves, and women gang raped, cruelly mutilated, and callously tossed aside. No one wanted to test the rumours.

Ah Thloo was prepared to defend her family. Before Ah Dang left, he had bought a rifle and a handgun and had taught her and his mother how to shoot. Together, they had drilled the family on emergency procedures. He had built a small room on the balcony: with openings reinforced by iron bars on all sides, it served as a secure lookout. There was room for a small table, stools, separate buckets for water and night soil, and enough floor space to accommodate several sleeping people. A woven bamboo mat, rolled up when not in use, served as a floor covering and mattress. A mosquito net hung in a corner, waiting to be spread out as needed.

Ah Thloo had included her neighbour, Ah Chiang Hoo, the wife of Ah Ngay Gonge's youngest brother, in the security plans. Ah Chiang Hoo was to come across the lane and into the house as soon as she heard the warning calls. Although a number of years older than Ah Thloo, she had a son the same age as Ah Lai. Her husband was in Montreal, smoking away his meagre earnings on his opium pipe. Unlike his elder brother, Ah Ngay Gonge, he was a reluctant worker, a neglectful husband, and an indifferent father. While he had left some money behind for his wife when he had last visited, no one could recall when he had ever sent a remittance from Canada. But no matter her circumstances, his wife was always cheerful. Not the brightest of women, she had no guile, nor a mosquito's worth of common sense; everyone in the family knew she needed looking after.

Ah Chiang Hoo and her young son scratched out a living from the kindness of their relatives. She hoarded every scrap, never knowing when it might come in handy, and her house resembled a garbage dump. Her hands and fingernails were deeply etched in black, and she exuded a strong odour, as if the neighbourhood cats and dogs had marked her as part of their territory. Ah Lai was careful never to accept food from *this* neighbour's house.

One night, the alarm was raised. Quietly and efficiently, the people in Ah Thloo's household attended to their jobs—barring all the windows, gathering food and fresh water, and locking themselves in the safe room. Ah Thloo had her weapons ready as she and her mother-in-law walked the perimeter of the lookout, peering out into the gloom, alert to any movement or unusual noise. Ah Chiang Hoo was late, but they were used to that, frustrating as it was; she was just not able to function quickly. They had left the front door unlocked for her.

Ah Chiang Hoo had heard sounds of hastily closed doors and barring shutters and had eventually surmised that something was going on. As usual, she came to ask Ah Thloo to explain things. Holding her son's shoulder with one hand, Ah Chiang Hoo waved aloft a kerosene lantern in the other, its bright yellow flame creating a sure target of her head.

"Ah Thloo, where are you?" she shouted from downstairs in her heavy Hien Gong village accent. "Everything is so dark!"

Ah Thloo whispered back, "Ah Chiang Hoo, please be quiet. Quickly, come upstairs." She told Ah Lai to run downstairs to intercept the mother and son before another word could be uttered, extinguish the deadly light, bar the door, and lead them upstairs into the refuge. It was pitch-black in the shuttered house, and the next few minutes were tense as the older woman stubbed her toes on every step up to the second floor, accompanied each time by a loud yelp, then a whispered apology.

A long, sleepless night was spent in Ah Chiang Hoo's malodorous company. Every once in a while, she would forget why they were there and try to talk. It was her son's job to stop her. They were all thankful when the red sky indicated dawn, and a runner from the neighbouring village gave the "all safe" signal, releasing them from their self-imposed captivity.

Ah Lai, growing up as she did through the war years, knew about working hard for scraps of food and the fear of her small hamlet being invaded by the Japanese. She also grew up with the certainty of her grandmother's devotion and her parents' love for her.

During the war with Japan, it was a rare event, but whenever the blue, self-sealing airmail envelopes from abroad, addressed in English and Chinese, arrived at their door, her mother would study the message first and then call her daughter to her side. Ah Lai was required to listen to her father's words as if they were commandments from on high.

> *You must work hard.*
> *You must obey your mother.*
> *You must mind your grandmother.*
> *Do not waste the hard-earned money Ah Yea sends you.*

Not surprisingly, he was very consistent. In a world of uncertainty, she was comforted by this and had memorized his words. Although he had never written, "I love you, daughter," she knew, simply by the fact that he sent instructions, that she was in his thoughts. She was part of him.

She was tall for a girl; she had probably inherited her height from her maternal grandmother, whom she called Ah Hoo, Mother's Mother. She had a dimple when she smiled, but she seldom did in those years. She was often hungry, and tired from working in the fields. Her eyes were big, honest, and frank. She observed everything but said little.

In a hamlet dominated by young boys, Ah Lai was the eldest of the girls. When she was young, they all played together, dug and built things in the dirt, tossed coins, climbed trees, and jumped ditches, all under the careful scrutiny of her paternal grandmother, whom she called Ah Ngange, Father's Mother. She had to be home every day by midafternoon.

Not long after Ah Dang returned to Canada, Ah Thloo bought a *sandoy*, hillock, little more than a bump in the land, not far from the hamlet. Ah Thloo, her mother-in-law, and even Ah Moydoy, had to work, planting staples like yams, soybeans, red beans, sorghum, and squash. Water had to be toted up in wooden buckets on a carrying-pole. It was arduous work.

They built a small hut there, where they could rest, sheltered from the sun, and eat their lunch. They also dug a secret cavern away from the hut, as a safe hiding place, and when the crops were almost ready for harvesting, Ah Thloo and her mother-in-law took turns sleeping there overnight, with a gun by their side. While Ah Lai was very young, one of the women had to stay home with her, as neither of them trusted Ah Moydoy to take care of the child on her own.

A typical day started just before sunrise. By the time Ah Lai was five or six, she was working in the vegetable garden with the women. Mostly, she *chan taw*, weeded, between the plants, and *haw taw*, gathered hay. When she was older, she also harvested fresh, sharp-edged weeds from the pond for pig feed; the scars from that task would not fade for decades. Back at home in the evenings, the adults occupied themselves with food preparation. Afterwards, they might take advantage of the early evening light to mend their rags. Ah Lai fed the livestock and swept the floors. With animals living in the house, the floors were often wet and slippery from their droppings.

During the war, Ah Thloo received no mail from Canada. She had no more cash, and inflationary prices made it impossible to buy anything, even rice. For a time, she got rice from her mother's farm, in exchange for working in the older woman's fields. They had two rice harvests a year. For some reason, the arrangement broke down and Ah Thloo was no longer welcomed. Ah Lai was only a child but she was very astute and was appalled when she realized, *Ah Hoo actually looks down on Ah Ma because she is so poor!*

Long after the war, Ah Thloo learned that Ah Dang had actually sent a total amount of fifty thousand yuan (more than three thousand dollars) in remittances over this period; not a penny ever reached her. The money must have gone somewhere. It could have been intercepted by the KMT government, which desperately needed cash; the Japanese might have stopped any foreign mail in an attempt to control intelligence; or the postman could have just pocketed it. Corruption was widespread. So was inefficiency. The country's infrastructure was in chaos and the postal service was not exempt.

Ah Thloo had no choice but to sell most of the gold jewellery from her wedding. With it, she bought seed. She made an agreement with Ah Ngay Gonge's wife and son-in-law, Ah Siew Sook, to share the seeds, supplies, work, and harvests. Ah Thloo's household also shared every meal they had with his family, until Gai Fong, the 1949 Revolution.

The times between harvests were the most difficult. Even cooking oil had to be used sparingly. Through careful conservation, their single barrel of cooking oil lasted several years, almost to the end of the eight-year war with Japan. Each autumn, Ah Lai harvested bamboo, which she cut into strips. Occasionally, she would weave the strips into baskets, but most of the time, the bamboo would be bundled tightly with straw and sold in the market town of Vak Sa Hui.

One day, after selling something in the market, Ah Lai found herself standing in front of a stall selling faan, cooked rice, and just staring, mesmerized by the smell, her mouth drooling, and hoping her mother would spend a few of their newly earned coins on the simple food. Instead, without a word, her mother gently guided her away from the temptation. Both walked away, crying silently. Both were starving, but only Ah Thloo understood they did not have enough money. On another occasion, Ah Thloo did buy a small bowl of rice, and smiling wanly, she watched as her daughter ate it all, every last grain.

They had no kerosene or oil for lighting, so they made their own torches by shaving the bamboo stems into fine pieces, bundling them onto the end of foot-long rods, and dipping the bamboo end into boiled pine resin. The resulting light was smoky and smelly, but it was better than being left in the dark.

o   o   o

AH LAI: CHINA, 1945

When Ah Lai was on her mission to petition her maternal grandmother for raw rice, just enough to tide the family over until the harvest, three weeks later, she saw not only the house filled to the rafters with bags of the grain, but she also noticed a whole cooked chicken on the kitchen table, cut up and ready to eat. The smell was unforgettable, but just looking at it made her empty guts twist in pain and grumble in protest. She took these sights as positive signs.

But she must have misinterpreted them. Ah Lai could not remember who told her "No," because her grandmother, her younger uncle, and his wife were all in the room. As soon as she understood they weren't going to give her anything, her face burned so hot she could not hear another word. She ran out of the house and into her mother's arms, and all she could do was sob.

Mother and daughter left just as they had come—empty-handed. And heavy-hearted. Ah Lai had not even been offered a chicken leg. It was a humiliation and a foo, bitter disappointment, borne by Ah Thloo for the rest of her life. All the fear, starvation, and deprivation they had suffered throughout that period were nothing compared to what had just happened. They had been totally abandoned by Ah Thloo's own family.

But Ah Thloo was undaunted. A person has to have *jee hay*, to take personal responsibility, and that is what she did. She organized everyone in the hamlet to harvest some of the unripened grains and pound them down to make a watery jook, gruel, to eat. They also scrounged the countryside for edible greens, eating whatever they could find.

Throughout the war with Japan, the Communists continued to build their peasant-based support by encouraging economic production, making sure their soldiers were friendly and helpful, providing organized transportation, and recruiting farmer activists to become new leaders. They worked out plans for land reform and land redistribution—plans that would eventually affect Ah Thloo.

The common front between the KMT and the CCP lasted until 1940. The KMT took a deliberately passive approach toward fighting the foreign invaders and again concentrated on attacking the CCP, whose efforts were focused on ousting the Japanese.

Japan then looked for other parts of the world to dominate and, in conjunction with Germany and Italy, fought in the Second World War. Because of its ongoing war with Japan, China was considered an Allied member. When the Axis lost the war in 1945, Japan capitulated to China.

o   o   o

V-J Day! Victory! Against Japan! The enemy had finally surrendered, and not only to the Allies, but to China as well! What a time to rejoice!

Ah Dang, then working as a waiter at the Lotus Garden Café on Clark Street in Chinatown, joined the crowds on the streets—to celebrate, to grieve, and to breathe a concerted sigh of relief. A few days later he lined up with the five-deep crowd of Chinese and whites to watch a parade. The streets were decorated with British and Chinese flags as well as silk banners and garlands of flowers. A temporary gate was constructed across Lagauchetière Street, hung with a banner proclaiming "V-J Day Celebration by the Chinese Community of Montreal" in both Chinese and English and festooned with flags, ribbons, and lanterns. Later, Ah Dang read that similar parades had been held in Chinatowns across the country, from Victoria, British Columbia, to Halifax, Nova Scotia.

When he heard that postal and telegraph services to China were open once more, his first action was to send a telegram to Ah Thloo. He waited anxiously for her response. Although he was not a religious man, he had been baptized in 1936 and now attended church to ask God to intervene on his behalf. So many people had died, of injuries from the war, torture, suicide, and starvation. He had not heard anything from China in years. Then . . . joy and thanksgiving, they were alive! He immediately wired money, hoping it would be enough; he had been reading about runaway inflation in China.

Throughout the war years, Ah Dang had joined other Chinese Canadians to aid their homeland. They raised funds for every imaginable military purpose, from airplanes to winter uniforms. In addition, until Ah Dang was certain that nothing was getting through, he had tried to send money to his family.

He also bought Canadian Victory Loan Second World War bonds. The combined purchases by the Chinese community, worth ten million dollars, were proportionally larger than those of any other ethnic group. His countrymen also had more tangible ways to help Canada's war effort. They worked in shipyards and factories and served as air-raid wardens. Farmers made a great effort to produce more food for Canadian troops overseas. And while Ah Dang was too old and too flat-footed to sign up, he'd read that Chinese communities across Canada contributed more than five hundred soldiers to the armed forces, a large proportion of whom were decorated for bravery.

In 1942, Canada and other Western nations negotiated to terminate the Unequal Treaties, to make China an equal partner and a Great Power in the world community. Canada, with a consulate in Nanjing since 1931, established under the auspices of the Japanese, upgraded diplomatic relations in 1943 to ambassador status, independent of Japan. Chinese consulates were opened in Toronto, Winnipeg, and Vancouver. China was gaining recognition as a sovereign nation.

New commercial agreements were signed between the two countries. Canada was already exporting wheat, flour, timber, clothing, electrical appliances, machinery, and foodstuffs. As China was still engaged in a civil war in 1947, Canada provided a loan of sixty million dollars (US) to China to buy surplus Canadian war equipment.

Chinese Canadians called for equal treatment under Canadian law as an earned right; the United States had repealed its anti-Chinese immigration laws in 1943. In recognition of their patriotism, Chinese servicemen were given the vote by BC after the war.

A number of other factors helped the Chinese gain acceptance in Canada. One was gambling, a double-edged sword. Over the years, while it had brought controversy and grief, it had also enabled the Chinese to raise the monies they did. Some of it even went to good use. Not only did gambling revenues fund the war effort, but the Chinese also built and maintained their own community-support systems. But over time, with the numbers of families increasing, even the Chinese drifted away from gambling, and instead, lottery tickets were sold to raise funds, seemingly a more acceptable form of gambling.

Another important consideration was that Canadian-born Chinese were seen to assimilate. By 1931, 75 per cent of the teenaged population had been born in Canada. In Montreal, they tended to be English speaking and attend church, and more were living in neighbourhoods outside Chinatown than in it.

Moving away from laundries and restaurants, Chinese worked as mechanics and machinists, as well as truck and taxi drivers. They owned small-scale manufacturing enterprises. Even Chinese women were gaining employment—many in the textile industry, but also as secretaries, bookkeepers, and clerks. There was also an emerging professional class of practising architects, engineers, physicians, dentists, and bank managers.

In May 1947, the Chinese Immigration Act of 1923 was finally repealed. That same year, BC granted the franchise to all Chinese and East Indians (the Japanese had to wait another year). The Canadian Citizenship Act came into effect as well, defining the right to vote as part of citizenship.

With these changes, Ah Dang had more reasons to rejoice, but his joy was short-lived. He learned that in China, the government had passed a Citizenship Law in 1929. Based on the principle of *jus sanguinis,* it meant that a child born anywhere in the world of a Chinese father was a citizen of China. The applicant had to have written permission from the Chinese minister of the interior before Canada could consider the immigration of his children. Ah Dang had looked forward to the day when he would see his family in the country he had chosen, but the process was delayed yet again.

With the Chinese political situation in disarray, Ah Dang decided to go directly to the source for the necessary documents. As a testament to his love for his family, his tenacity, and his sense of adventure, he braved the battle lines between the Nationalists and Communists to return to Longe Gonge Lay in the spring of 1947.

He landed in Shanghai, which had suffered under Japanese oppression since 1932. The city was in ruins and its streets were filled with orphans, refugees, and beggars who clamoured for coins, reaching out, crying plaintively, exposing their scars and lost limbs, and touching his clothing. When he gave money to one person, others swarmed him.

They all want something from me, but there are just too many. How can I give to this one but not that one? he thought. All he could do was close his ears, harden his heart, and walk away.

o   o   o

AH LAI: CHINA, 1945–47

Miraculously, a telegram arrived at Ah Lai's house in 1945. Later, a blue aerogram and a wire of money followed. The letter contained instructions from her father, especially for her!

Now that the war is over, you should go to school.
Some of this money is for you to buy new clothes.

Ah Lai did not know which was more exciting—going to school for the first time or choosing a new piece of fabric. She had watched the boys with envy as they studied their books and walked around reciting texts. Her former playmates called her stupid because she was a girl and couldn't go to school.

Two new outfits! She had patched, repatched, extended, and re-extended her hand-me-downs over the last eight years. New clothes were a novelty, more like an unforgettable luxury.

Ah Thloo enrolled her daughter in a one-room schoolhouse in the nearby village. Ah Lai was smart, and although she was older than most of the other children, she caught up to her grade in no time. But the children still teased her and followed her home, taunting her, so after six months, she asked her mother to move her to another school farther away.

Ah Ngange woke her up every morning at 5:00 AM, made her breakfast, and accompanied her to the new school. In the afternoon, she came back to walk her granddaughter home. There were no problems with the school children there. Ah Lai excelled and from then on always came first or second in her class. Unfortunately, there was only money enough for two more years of education.

When the Communist troops arrived in the southern countryside in 1946, Ah Thloo saw that they treated the peasant farmers very differently from any other military people. The soldiers were actually helpful. Rather than plunder and steal, they worked beside her and her neighbours. When they talked about land reform and land redistribution, they explained it in simple terms, though the ideas sounded too good to be true. Still, Ah Thloo was intrigued and was soon recognized as someone with intelligence and ability. Her education helped, as did her reputation as a brave defender of the hamlet. She was given the job of coordinating county land registry and measurements, which involved identifying the owners of each piece of land and determining its size and boundaries. While others on her team surveyed the plots, she checked the accuracy of the information about ownership from the fragmented government records against reports from local villagers. She worked throughout the county of Hoyping, which comprises approximately seventeen hundred square kilometres, and was often required to be away from home for days at a time.

While Ah Thloo was away, Ah Lai became increasingly dependent on Ah Ngange. At the age of twelve she got the measles. Although she was taller than her grandmother by then, for months afterwards, Ah Lai was piggybacked everywhere, as coddled as a baby.

Later that year, she would lose an important part of her childhood.

Should sons be born to him
They will be put to slumber on couches
They will be clad in robes
They will have sceptres to play with
They will be resplendent with knee covers
The future ruler, the prince of the land
—H.J. Hsia, *The Fair Sex in China:*
They Lift Up Half the Sky

EIGHT

Father Rejoices

AH LAI: CHINA, 1947

At twelve, Ah Lai was to meet her father for the first time since she was a baby. She was excited and at the same time very anxious. She had no idea how to act with him—he was her father, the sender of commandments.

The family knew he was coming; they just didn't know exactly when he would be arriving in the hamlet. The women had scrubbed the house clean and replaced the old, patched bed linens with the ones Ah Thloo had made as part of her trousseau.

Then it rained steadily for a week. It was monsoon season, and the house was flooded with brown muddy water, partway up the stairs. All the furniture and animals had to be lugged up to the second floor. The only benefit was that there were fresh fish swimming inside the house.

Ah Thloo used to say to Ah Lai, "Don't go to the market. Your father doesn't like it," and she had taken the instruction to heart. During the war with Japan, they had rarely had the opportunity to shop, but with her father's

103

recent remittances, she and her mother were stocking the larder in readiness for his homecoming. Although the civil war was still being waged in the north, the markets in the south had access to goods smuggled through the ports in Guangzhou. Things could be found, if one had enough money.

Unfortunately, Ah Dang's arrival coincided with Ah Thloo and Ah Lai's return from another day of shopping.

"Ah Dang, your wife and daughter are back from the market!" Ah Chiang Hoo shouted excitedly. "See how big your daughter has grown!"

"Umm," he murmured from over the balcony.

Ah Lai heard the exchange between their well-meaning neighbour and the hidden male voice she surmised was her father's. Oh, why did Ah Chiang Hoo have to tell him *that*? Although she had bought nothing for herself, she had been caught shopping: she had unwittingly disobeyed one of his commandments, and he would be angry with her. It wasn't her fault; they had bought thlonge, food, for *him*! Ah Lai's heart, already racing from the prospect of seeing her father, immediately sank to her stomach, making her nauseous and faint.

Her mother pushed her forward, saying, "Go say hello to your father."

Ah Lai's legs shook all the way up the stairs. When she saw him, the only words that came out of her dry mouth were a croaky "Ah Yea." Then she fled into Ah Ngange's room, slammed the door behind her, threw herself onto the bed, and sobbed her heart out.

o   o   o

AH DANG

Ah Dang had had to hire a boat in the nearest market town to take him to the flooded hamlet. The first person he met when he arrived was the neighbour, Ah Chiang Hoo, who greeted him enthusiastically, hailing him from an upstairs window in her house. When he acknowledged her shout with a wave of his hand, she continued to blather loudly at him. Perhaps she hoped he was bringing her a remittance from her husband. Unfortunately, he wasn't, but Ah Ngay Gonge had given him some money to give her. "Don't tell her it's from me," he had said. "Let her believe it's from my brother."

Inside the house, he was pleasantly surprised to be welcomed by his mother, Ah Tew May. While there was no look of happiness on her face, she called out his name and helped him unload the boat. In the past, she had ignored his greeting and his presence for as long as possible.

Each time he brought up a load of his belongings, he heard Ah Chiang Hoo carrying on. It did not matter that he did not actually converse with her. He could hear her above the slapping of the water and the clunking of the steering pole used by the boatman. He knew about the unpleasant odour that accompanied her and was grateful that the flood prevented her from actually visiting. Not wanting to be impolite, he gave her an occasional grunt. Raising her voice even higher, she announced the return of his wife and daughter from the market.

He quickly returned to the bedroom to check himself in the mirror, making sure he looked presentable. He wanted to make a good first impression on his daughter. When she came up the stairs to greet him, he was surprised and pleased to see how tall and pretty she had grown.

Opening his arms to embrace her, he was happy to hear her call him "Ah Yea." She was the first person ever to call him "Father," but he did not get to hug her, for she immediately ran into the room across the hall and slammed the door shut. What had just happened?

o　o　o

AH THLOO

This time, Ah Thloo had looked forward to her husband's arrival. She wanted him to know how smart and well behaved their daughter was, to see the hill-ock she owned, and to recognize her new status as a leader in the area. She now headed a land redistribution committee. She was disappointed when he did not pay the close attention she had expected.

"All in good time. First, I want to take you away from all of this. You've worked hard to keep everyone alive through a horrible time and you deserve to be rewarded," Ah Dang said.

He took her to Guangzhou, where he bought her new jewellery to replace some of the gold that had been sold during the war. He bought her exquisite pieces of translucent jade: two round disks and an oval cabochon. She had the disks made into earrings with screw-back clasps. The cabochon was fashioned into a ring. They shopped for fabric for their daughter, stocked up on herbs for their daily use, and bought a package of the best ginseng for his mother. It was in Guangzhou that their next child was conceived.

○　○　○

AH DANG AND AH THLOO: CHINA, 1947–1948

In Guangzhou, Ah Dang had attempted to get permission from the appropriate ministries for his daughter to emigrate to Canada when the time came, but frustratingly, all he got was a bureaucratic runaround.

Back in the hamlet, he tried to get to know his daughter. He wanted to establish a relationship with her before he left for Canada again, but it was difficult. She seemed reluctant to talk to him.

He tried smoothing the way by complimenting her. She had intelligent eyes and a bright smile, not that she ever smiled at him. He told her she looked like her mother. Women liked new things; he gave her gifts. From Canada, he had brought her a full-length woollen coat that fell in an elegant A-line. He had forgotten how hot it was in Guangdong. She always accepted her gifts with extreme politeness—she had been taught well by Ah Thloo—but she still appeared to be uncomfortable in his presence.

He asked her to take him to her school. At home, he had seen her workbooks; she had scored almost perfectly in every subject. He met her teacher, who spoke enthusiastically about his star pupil. Ah Dang was proud of her, but he did not show his pride to her teacher or his daughter, lest he be seen as boastful.

When he read her compositions, there were words he had forgotten and others he did not even recognize. In only two years of schooling, her education had surpassed his own. When he spoke to her again, to encourage her in her studies, he reverted to an old saying to hide his own lack of education: "*Kange nang woo joit*, study hard, avoid stupidity." Immediately, seeing her face turn from eagerness to stone, he realized he had said the wrong thing, but he did not know how to turn the situation around. They each retreated, neither knowing how to reach out to reconnect.

While Ah Dang was home, he went to the market every week to bring back special food. Roast pork with crackling was a favourite, especially when accompanied by *haam ha*, a salty fermented shrimp paste.

He also introduced the family to a miraculous medicine. Ah Dang travelled everywhere with his jar of Mentholatum Decongestant and Analgesic Ointment, advertised to help "relieve cold symptoms, chapped skin, and coughs." He used it to help clear his stuffy nose. When his daughter caught a cold and developed a cough, he had his mother rub it on the girl's chest and was relieved that it helped her to sleep through the night. Finally, he felt he had done something positive for Ah Lai.

Husband and wife carried on the topsy-turvy relationship that had become the pattern for their lives together. It did not seem to take much for one to be misunderstood and then the yelling would start. There was no more physical violence, from either one, but neither would let the other have the last word. However, while Ah Dang's anger would spark, flare, then die forgotten, Ah Thloo's would smoulder and simmer, to be dredged up and stoked over the years. It was her one demon. Whenever they argued, Ah Thloo refused to sleep with him; she stomped away and locked herself overnight in the lookout.

Normally, Ah Lai shared the bed with her mother, but while her father was in the hamlet, she went to sleep with Ah Ngange. Both she and her grandmother actually preferred this arrangement. Ah Ngange was always the same, whereas her mother seemed preoccupied and distant. Her father, in person, did not live up to the image Ah Lai had created as a child, listening to her mother read his letters. When her parents argued—and it was hard to miss the verbal volleys—she would cry herself to sleep while Ah Ngange comforted her.

As Ah Dang had done with his wife's first pregnancy, he again sought the services of the area's best physician. The pregnancy had no complications, so no plans were made to go to the hospital in town, and the birth took place at home, on their marriage bed. At the ages of forty-six and thirty-seven respectively, Ah Dang and Ah Thloo became the joyous parents of a son. He was born on the twenty-seventh day of the first month of the lunar calendar under the sign of the Boar. The year was 1948.

A son was every man's crowning desire; a son to carry on his name. The child attracted adoration, with large, dark brown eyes and a small bow of a mouth. He was a contented and quiet baby. His cries were no louder than a mew, more like a puppy in distress, so his grandmother nicknamed him *Gowdoy*, Puppy. His father picked him up as soon as the infant was awake. They would sit for hours together, the baby swaddled in a blanket and snuggled on his father's lap. His sister also cuddled and played with him when all the adults were occupied elsewhere, and until she went back to school, the siblings were inseparable.

Ah Thloo followed the traditional thirty-day lying-in period after the birth and, as she had done after Ah Lai was born, watched the baby like a hungry hawk. She feasted her eyes on his beauty, breathed in his smells, and felt his breath as her own. Sighing with relief at having produced a boy, she now made sure he thrived.

Ah Ngange made soups to nourish and restore her daughter-in-law's *yang*, hot energies, to counter the effects of the mainly *yin*, cold effects, dominant during pregnancy, according to traditional Chinese medicine. She slaughtered chickens, collected eggs, and sent Ah Dang to the market to buy whisky and ginger. Using ginger in copious quantities, she cooked the chicken in the whisky and added peanuts and a handful of dried *gim ja toy*, lily stalks, which she had rehydrated, knotted, and tossed in. Modern-day nutritionists might recognize these foods as adding protein to the mother's diet, but traditional practitioners note their ability to purify and thin the blood and rid the body of potentially harmful yin effects.

Neither the baby nor the mother went out of the house during that first month. It was a delicate time for the baby, and few people except the immediate family were allowed to visit, in case they brought disease. Many infants died, so this was deemed a necessary precaution. Both mother and child were to stay away from drafts, cold, wind, and dirty air. Thus, bathing and hair washing were forbidden, as cold could seep into a body when the skin was still damp and before hair could dry.

After the month was up, the family held a Choot Ngiet Gat How, one-month head-shaving celebratory meal, to which everyone in the hamlet and all their relatives and friends were invited. At their first glimpse of the baby, everyone clucked and chuckled with delight. No one who held him willingly passed him on to anyone else.

The most typical baby present was *lie see*, money wrapped in red paper, red being the colour for happiness and celebration. During that time, when few people had money, they gave small, practical items, such as a homemade hat or a hand-carved toy, decorated with the appropriate colour.

All the guests helped themselves to red-dyed hard-boiled eggs and *yuon*, a doughy confection made from sticky rice flour and brown sugar, rolled

Showing off a new son, 1948.
UNKNOWN PHOTOGRAPHY STUDIO, CHINA

into small balls and steamed. Eggs, considered a delicacy, symbolized life and fertility. The roundness of the eggs and the yuon symbolized continuity, harmony, and a happy life; the Chinese word for round is *yuon*. Also served was a soup made of pork knuckles simmered in dark, sweet vinegar. Ah Dang, having been influenced by Montreal friends from Guangzhou, added ginger and hard-boiled eggs to the soup. He had scoured the market for delicacies, sparing no expense, and bought whatever was available for the feast.

Choot Ngiet Gat How was also the time to name the child; after a month, its chances for survival were increased. Ah Dang and Ah Thloo agreed on the name Yuet Wei, meaning "the Most Accomplished in all Guangdong Province." They presented the infant to the ancestors' altar, where incense burned. There, Ah Wei's downy hair was shaved, except for three square patches, one on top and one on each side of his little head: his first haircut, symbolizing his independent existence.

Ah Dang took his family to the photographer's shop. Though it was rare in portraits of the time, almost everyone was smiling, though it was hard to tell with Ah Ngange. Rejoicing, relieved, happy, contented, and satisfied were the emotions shown on the respective faces of the father, the mother, the big sister, the baby, and the grandmother.

The baby's bottom was naked. What better way to show off a son! What more needed to be said?

Applicant arrived in Canada 11th Oct., 1921 on the "SS" [*sic*] *Empress of Japan*, Port of Vancouver, BC. From Port of Entry he remained in Vancouver for eight years, then proceeded to Montreal, Que. . . . He made three trips to China for a total of three years and two months out of Canada, the last trip being from March 1947 to June 1948 and on his first trip he married in China . . . Chinese Immigration Certificate checked and found in order. Sponsors appear to be of good character and are not known or suspected of having any subversive tendencies toward the State.

—S/Cst. E.H. Desaulniers, Royal Canadian Mounted Police

NINE

Father Regroups

AH DANG: MONTREAL, 1949–53

During the voyage back to Canada, the photo of his son kept Ah Dang's spirits buoyed, despite the emptiness he was feeling. *This separation will be harder than the other two because I now have a son!*

When his first child was born, she had been an unexpected surprise and delight. She could make him laugh out loud just by curling her little hands around his pinkie; he had created a family of his own. Now he had a son. He had never known he could feel this way about a child who still could not talk or walk; he felt invincible!

Thinking about his boy, he could almost, but not quite, forget his bafflement regarding his daughter. On this last visit, when she was certainly old enough to talk sensibly, he had not understood her reaction to him.

111

He had tried hard to let her get to know him, but it was almost as if she was afraid of him. *What was there to be afraid of?* he wondered. While he was in the hamlet, he had never laid a hand on her in anger nor ever raised his voice.

He had watched her from a distance as she interacted with other adults. With them, she was chatty, easygoing, even happy, and he especially noticed how affectionately she treated her Ah Ngange. Yet whenever he spoke to her, she was reluctant to talk to him and tended to respond in single words, even after a whole year of living in the same house. He was proud of her though; she was always first or second in school. She was a smart one.

He thought about Ah Thloo. He did not know what he had done to deserve such a difficult wife. He had long ago learned that beating her did not change her—it only made her more *ngang giang*, stiff-necked and stubborn. He had given it up. He recognized and admired her gumption.

He himself had learned to fight when he first came to Canada. The British Columbia fishing and logging camps, where he had worked as a cook, attracted rough, tough *guey law*, devil or ghost men, hooligans. Living together in close quarters and away from civilization made them feel like prisoners, and they needed a diversion to vent their feelings. A Chink was an easy target. He was a Chink, sometimes the only one in the camp.

The first time he was picked on and beaten, he was afraid to fight back and had to stay in bed for two days, losing wages, before he could resume work. He vowed it would never happen again. The next time he was in town on leave, he bought a knuckle-duster and a leather sap, both of which he learned to use effectively, and he never left home without his protection. The hooligans got as good as they gave. Soon, Ah Dang had a reputation for being tough, earning him some grudging respect among the whites.

Ah Thloo was like that, much like Scarlett O'Hara in his favourite movie, *Gone with the Wind*. He had gone to the theatre to watch it at least thirteen times. Scarlett was feisty too: single-minded in getting what she wanted and not bending to anyone's will. Fearless. His little wife had saved the village from bandit raids *and* the Japanese, if the stories he had heard from the neighbours were true. He believed them. He would believe anything they said about Ah Thloo. She would never boast about it to him, but he knew she was capable. That was why he wanted to keep her. He would never abandon her for another because he knew they were so much alike. He had been right to choose her.

But she could make him so angry! It took just a few well-chosen words, and his blood boiled so much that he felt his eyes popping out of his head like those fancy goldfish sold in the market. She had learned from that poisoned-tongued viper, his mother, after all. *But I don't want to think about my mother*, and he shook his head to get her image out of his mind.

On this last trip to China, he had stayed away as long as he dared, fifteen months—by far the longest time he had been out of Canada. He entered his adopted country at the port of Sarnia, Ontario, on June 6, 1948. For the first time, he was not detained and humiliated by immigration officials upon landing on the shores of his chosen home, nor was he required to show his head tax receipt. Rather than being herded off, he disembarked at his leisure with the other passengers and went on his way, just like a white person. Just like a human being. It felt good!

o · o · o

More than ever before, Ah Dang was eager to have his family join him in Canada. He had not been able to watch his daughter grow up, and now she was a stranger to him; he did not want that to happen with his son. For a time, he kept trying to apply for permission from the Chinese government for his children to join him, but in the spring of 1949, he decided to work at getting his Canadian citizenship. He had lived in the country for twenty-five years, thus establishing himself as a resident.

The process entailed eight steps and took almost two years. The first step was for Ah Dang to submit a Declaration of Intention. The purpose of this was to show how and when he had arrived in Canada, list his trips back and forth to China, indicate identifying marks on his person, and provide information about his family. His signature on the form indicated his willingness to renounce any allegiance to any foreign sovereign or state. On May 25, 1949, the form was notarized by a justice of the peace. The declaration had to be accompanied by two other corroborating documents: a memo from a commissioner of the Immigration Branch, to confirm Ah Dang's original date and port of entry into Canada, which took a month to be processed; and a confidential report by the Royal Canadian Mounted Police (RCMP), which took two months. The RCMP conducted an investigation and interviews with Ah Dang, as well as with two "prominent British subjects" who vouched for the applicant and confirmed he was recognized as "being of good character."

Not unlike banns for a marriage in some churches, the Canadian Citizenship Act required the declaration to be posted at the courthouse in a public and "conspicuous place" for three months. This was done starting August 25, 1949.

However, it was not until a year later, on August 8, 1950, that a Petition for Citizenship, in which the applicant "humbly prays" that a Certificate of Citizenship be issued to him and to his minor children, was granted by Judge J.G. Magnan. Ten days later, the petition, attesting to the fact that Ah Dang was "a fit and proper person to be naturalized," was forwarded to the Minister of Citizenship and Immigration for a final decision. Approval by the Registrar of Canadian Citizenship was granted on November 26, 1950. On January 26, 1951, Ah Dang finally became a Canadian citizen, swearing true allegiance to His Majesty King George the Sixth.

o   o   o

By the 1950s, Montreal was bustling, becoming the country's financial centre. Quebec was attracting workers to its growing industrial sector. In the latter half of the decade many in the Chinese community were bringing their wives and children, so the province's Chinese population rose from 1,904 to 4,794, most of it concentrated in Montreal.

When Ah Dang was in China, he had listened to the locals and the townsfolk discussing the civil war. While he was careful about what he said, to whom he said it, and within whose hearing he spoke, he gained enough information to make a choice. He had been a strong supporter of Dr. Sun Yat-sen and the Kuomintang Party, and although he had not joined any political associations in the Chinatowns of Canada, he had purchased bonds and donated to the local KMT chapter. But he was outraged when, soon after the Japanese surrender in 1945, General Jiang had used Japanese soldiers to fight the Communists. That action had made him stop donating to the KMT Party.

When Ah Dang had last been in China, he had seen the widespread corruption and carpet-bagging greediness of KMT officials. In seeking a solution to his children's immigration situation, he had given the suggested bribes, but still, nothing had happened. The KMT's economic policies, intended to curb runaway inflation, were disastrous. In 1937, a hundred yuan could purchase two oxen; by 1949, it could buy only a sheet of paper. In 1948, when the KMT attempted a currency reform measure to create the "gold yuan," prices rose eighty-five thousand times within a six-month period. Ah Dang held little hope for a continuing government under the KMT.

He could have stayed neutral, for he had chosen Canada as his country, but he had to safeguard his family in China, in case, for whatever unthinkable reason, they could never join him. He decided to learn more about the Communists for himself, so, on his last trip, he had attended some of Ah Thloo's meetings and work parties.

Ah Thloo had told him how different the Communists were from any other soldiers who had come through the countryside, hardworking and helpful. Ah Thloo introduced him to some of the Communist soldiers. As they did not wear uniforms, but the same clothes as the locals, it was at first hard to distinguish them. However, as Ah Dang watched, he noticed an aura of authority about them, indicating training and discipline. They looked genuine to him.

Having been a victim of the peasant feudal system, he could see the positive intent of, and benefits being produced by, the land reform program. By sharing tools, seed, and labour, his family and neighbours also shared in the diversity of the harvests. Perhaps China had a future with the Chinese Communist Party in government. He made his first donation to the CCP before he left China.

Back in Canada, Ah Dang followed the progress of the Communist People's Liberation Army in the civil war. Significant battles continued in key locations, including Beijing, Nanjing, the KMT capital, and Chengdu, to which Jiang retreated after resigning as president of China on January 21, 1949. On October 1, 1949, Mao Zedong proclaimed the founding of the People's Republic of China. On December 10, 1949, Jiang left China for Taiwan.

Following the formation of the People's Republic of China, the Chinese newspapers reported that many well-to-do citizens were fleeing to Hong Kong and Macau, where living conditions were far from ideal. Relatives in foreign countries feared that China's new collectivist principles meant that

Chinese war bond.

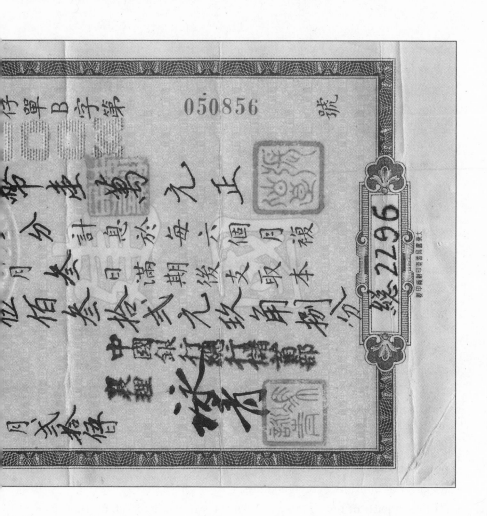

much-needed remittances would be confiscated, but Ah Dang did not have to worry on that account. He had left Ah Thloo the bulk of his savings, and he knew she would keep the money safe and spend it wisely. But he needed her and their children here. Armed with his new citizenship rights, he set about bringing his family to Canada.

o o o

AH THLOO: CHINA, 1949–1952

The war is over! Have you heard—the war is over?! The joyous cries were almost as ubiquitous as the greeting "Have you eaten rice yet?" Especially in Tiananmen Square.

Built during the Ming Dynasty, Tiananmen, the Gate of Heavenly Peace, is where imperial edicts were issued or announcements of great import made. On October 1, 1949, Mao Zedong stood on the viewing balcony of the gate to hoist up the new flag of China—five gold stars on a sea of red—and declared the founding of the People's Republic of China. Below, on the square, thousands of people cheered, waving banners, lanterns, and scarves. Beijing was once again the capital.

Earlier that day, Mao was appointed chairman of both the Central People's Government and the People's Revolutionary Military Committee. Zhou Enlai was appointed premier of the Central People's Government Council and minister of foreign affairs.

In most parts of the country, a collective sigh was exhaled; outright battles would now stop. However, pockets of resistance by KMT forces and their sympathizers would continue to be a problem for the next few years.

From 1949 to 1952, the Central People's Government concentrated on rehabilitating the national economy. The state seized control of everything. Private businesses were condemned, and their owners, if they had not managed to flee the country, were in jeopardy. The state took over customs, banks, mines, factories, and transportation systems. Inflation was brought under control. Supplies of basic necessities, such as food, cotton, cloth, coal, and salt, and staples such as grain and seed were all centralized. Transportation systems, including railways, shipping lines, and roads, were revived.

More importantly in the countryside, the government took over all the land and private property. Landlords, considered corrupt and a bane to peasants, were stripped of their wealth and persecuted. Although Ah Thloo and her parents had owned land, they had worked it and not leased it to others, so they were not considered landlords.

In fact, Ah Thloo worked on the land redistribution project, helping to ensure that landless tenants and the poorest peasants gained the most while absentee landlords lost the most. Groups of poor peasants gathered together to celebrate the burning of their rental bills, which had been charged in produce and disguised as taxes and duties. By 1952, more than three hundred million peasants had received forty million hectares of land and were exempted from rents of more than thirty-five billion kilograms of grain.

It is not now known how much land Ah Thloo and her family received in the redistribution, but it was soon irrelevant. By then, Ah Lai had returned to school, this time to a boarding school. Soon afterwards, her family experienced a drastic shift.

And the angel said unto them, Fear not: for, behold, I bring you good tidings of great joy, which shall be to all people.

For unto you is born this day in the city of David a Saviour, which is Christ the Lord.

And suddenly there was with the angel a multitude of the heavenly host praising God and saying,

Glory to God in the highest, and on earth peace, good will toward men.

—Luke 2:10-11, 13-14

TEN

First Christmas

AH THLOO: ALASKA, DECEMBER 24, 1954

The airplane meal was distributed not long after the flight took off from Alaska. Ah Thloo did not recognize any of the food: there was some kind of dry white meat, a mound of white, mushy starch, some green peas, and a spoonful of red sauce, and covering everything was a grey-brown sauce. No rice. She tasted a bit of everything and found it was "edible—but only just," as Ah Tew May used to say about all of Ah Thloo's cooking. It was very bland, except for the red sauce, which she anticipated might be spicy but turned out to be sweet.

After the meal, the stewardesses gave everyone a small gift wrapped in bright, festive paper. Ah Wei got a toy, and Ah Thloo thought, *What a nice way to welcome us to Canada!*

o   o   o

It took some time for Ah Thloo to decide if she wanted to uproot herself and her family to start life anew in an alien environment. In China, she had established an independent life—quite an accomplishment for a woman. She had had to make life-and-death decisions; her family had remained intact and had survived famine, bandits, war, and revolution through her efforts. More recently, she was engaged in important work to improve the economic life of the community. People sought her opinions and her help; she had become a leader.

By 1953, she and Ah Dang had been married for almost a quarter-century, but they had spent less than five years together, much of it in conflict. Who would look forward to more of the same? However, she had to admit that he had tried harder than any other Gim San law she knew of to send money.

It was something in the first letter she received after the revolution that clinched her decision. Ah Dang told her he had received his citizenship, and could now legally apply for her and the children to go to Canada. He had told her he could not apply for his mother: Canada would not let her into the country. He also wrote, "Ah Thloo, you are my second life. I cannot go on without you." Finally, he had written her some *hiem wa*, sweet words. Perhaps he had changed.

She showed the letter to her daughter. Ah Lai had known for a long time of her father's wish for the family to join him in Canada. With his citizenship it was now possible and the declaration of love was making it more of a reality.

Ah Thloo felt it would be cruel to tell Ah Ngange (as she called her mother-in-law, now) that she had not been invited, but the older woman refused to go anyway, claiming, "I am seventy years old, too old to survive the long trip. I wouldn't last a day living in the country of *faan guey law*, foreign devils! I'm staying here. I'll die in my own home."

She had never spoken out against her son's wishes and his right to have his children join him in Canada. Ah Thloo knew Ah Ngange loved the children, and that the feelings were mutual. From a distance, she had watched them together; the older woman's voice became affectionate and she actually smiled when she was with them. As a child, Ah Lai had always run to Ah Ngange first when she came in from playing outdoors, and it was no different now. When she came home from boarding school or if she was upset, she sought solace from Ah Ngange first, then perhaps practical advice from Ah Thloo. Ah Wei, ever watchful of his sister's actions, followed suit.

While Ah Thloo had always envied their relationship, she was grateful for her mother-in-law's help in raising the children, and she was surprised but relieved when the older woman so adamantly refused to join them in going to Canada. In her own heart, Ah Thloo nursed a hope that perhaps away from Ah Ngange, she and the children could seal the gap between them.

They were all about to leave the village for the city of Guangzhou when Ah Lai went to her mother in tears. Ah Thloo thought she was feeling sad at having to leave Ah Ngange; she knew they were very close, but she didn't know how devoted until then.

"Ma-ma, please do not be angry at me for what I'm about to say."

"Ah Nui, what is it? You can tell me anything."

"I don't want to go to Canada."

"Don't be afraid. I know things will be different. But I promise, we'll be together. I'll spend more time with you."

"It's not that."

"What's the issue, then? You're still too young. How can I leave you behind?"

"Ma-ma, I'm eighteen years old. At this age you were married to Ah Yea."

"We are not talking about me. Times were different then."

"You know I want to marry Ah Haw One."

"Ah Yea should choose a husband for you!"

"I don't believe in that old-fashioned practice of blind marriage, and neither do you!"

This was true enough. Having been a victim of such a union, Ah Thloo had been actively promoting women's rights since the revolution, but she wasn't going to let her daughter catch her with that argument. However, she had met Ah Haw One many times and tacitly approved of her daughter's choice. She had worked with his mother on some of her committees, so she knew something of his background. His father was also a sojourner, to Southeast Asia.

"In Canada, life will be better. There're no famines or droughts, no food shortages."

Ah Ngange and Ah Lai, 1956.
UNKNOWN PHOTOGRAPHY STUDIO, CHINA

"How can life be better in a country that hates us? It has kept our family apart! In the four years since Gai Fong, our own lives have improved here. The murderous Japanese have been defeated. The warlords who roamed the country raping the land have been executed. Landlords no longer hold all the wealth in their corrupt hands. The people, peasants like us who work the land, now have rights and power."

It was a long speech, like something the girl had practised for a school recital. It reminded Ah Thloo of the long passages she had had to memorize during her few years at school. Inwardly, she agreed with everything her daughter had said and was proud that the girl had learned her history so well.

Ah Lai continued, her words tumbling out faster and faster, like hot pebbles burning her tongue. "I've just been accepted into college. I've worked to stay in first or second place at school! I can get a good education here. I want to help rebuild my country. This isn't the right time for me to leave! I can't even speak the language in Canada, and I'll be too old to start school all over again. My little brother will have his chance. You must go for his sake."

It was obvious her daughter had thought hard about this, and Ah Thloo could not find any fault in her reasoning. She was right: for four-year-old Ah Wei, everything was still new and no matter where he lived, he would adapt. He would also grow up living with his father, important for a boy.

Finally, Ah Lai said, "Also, there is Ah Ngange. It will break her heart to have her grandson taken away from her. I think she still needs me." Ah Thloo understood that her daughter had chosen Ah Ngange over her. It must have been as hard to say as it was to hear, but the decision had been made, and was to have long-term consequences.

After their discussion, Ah Thloo cried herself to sleep every night. Ah Lai was away at school. When she came home on the weekends, Ah Thloo acted as if everything was back to normal and never again brought up the subject of going to Canada.

Ah Thloo made plans to go to Guangzhou, where the Chinese emigration offices were located. She did not know how long it would take for the government to grant her and her son leave to emigrate, but Ah Dang had told her to anticipate a long wait, both in various offices, where she had to be interviewed in person, and between meetings, while decisions were being pondered.

Ah Dang had sent money to buy goods in the city, so Ah Thloo packed only what she could carry in one suitcase. There wasn't much from their lives in their home village that would be useful in Canada anyway. She took a change of clothing, the least faded and tattered of their belongings; they had been patched so often that even she couldn't tell what colour the original fabric had been.

She left all of the bed coverings she had so carefully embroidered for her wedding. Although they had been cleaned and stored away with mothballs, after almost a quarter-century, they too had inevitable stains and holes. Besides, they were too bulky to carry. Nothing from the kitchen either, except for their ivory chopsticks. Ah Ngange would need everything else.

Ah Thloo had let the neighbours know of their intention to leave, if not the exact date. Every family had had members leave, so it was not an unusual event. Still, everyone loved sweet little Ah Wei, and Ah Thloo's contributions to the county were well recognized; they would both be missed. Each neighbour family came to the house to say goodbye with gifts—folded paper packages of loose tea or herbs, trinkets for her son—and letters to their overseas relatives to be sent from Hong Kong.

Some of them, like her neighbour, Ah Chiang Hoo, would themselves be going to Montreal, so they would meet again there. Still, it was hard to say goodbye. Ah Thloo nodded when the families told her they would look after Ah Ngange, although she thought it more likely the old woman would be looking after them. *She* wasn't the person for whom Ah Thloo's heart was as heavy as a bushel of damp grain.

As for her own parents, Ah Thloo did not feel the need to bid them a final farewell. She had left their household when she married, and though she had visited them annually, she still felt ostracized by them. They had made that clear during the worst of the war with Japan, when they had denied Ah Thloo and her family food. Time enough to inform them of her move after she had settled in Canada.

On the evening before they left, Ah Thloo walked through the tiny hamlet, trying to memorize everything about the place she had called home for the past twenty-four years. As she strolled, the stand of tall houses already seemed to have turned their backs on her. All she could see were flickering yellow lights from kerosene lamps and kitchen cooking hearths, as the women, including Ah Ngange, prepared their evening meals. The smells of burning grass, firewood, and coal mixed with those of hot peanut oil, browning garlic, and soy sauce. The sudden crackle of oil indicated the addition of wet greens to a hot wok. She caught the pungent smell of *haam nguey*, dried salted fish, as it was steamed over rice, from several homes. From the bamboo garden, she heard the rustling of leaves and could imagine the bamboo swaying in unison as a breeze blew through it.

The children, including Ah Wei, were playing outside, climbing trees and chasing each other, or the chickens, dogs, and piglets, around the yard. Ah Thloo had not told the youngster anything about the trip. She did not want to upset him with the knowledge of parting from his beloved sister or grandmother. He played innocently, giggling, lighthearted, and happy among his friends.

The men sat on low stools outside their doors in the laneway, *gong goo-doy*, telling stories, or napping. Later, they would bring out their tea and water pipes and continue their men's gossip. After dinner, Ah Ngange helped Ah Wei get ready for bed; she would stay with him through the night. Ah Thloo washed the dishes and tidied up. Then she brought a three-legged wooden stool out to have a last chat with the *moin how*, front door, neighbour. There was nothing much more to say about the upcoming journey; they just talked about this and that to pass the evening. When Ah Thloo finally retired, she tossed and turned for a long time before falling into a restless sleep.

The three family members left home at dawn the next morning, quietly and without much fuss. They would need the time to make their connections. Ah Ngange insisted that she piggyback her grandson all the way to Hien Gong Huy, the market village, where the next part of the journey would take place. He did not protest; he loved to ride on her back whenever he had the chance. She did not need to use the via aie, baby sling, to carry him. "That's for babies!" he had protested. "I'm big now!" He hung on tightly, wrapping his arms around her neck and his legs all the way around. Her torso was so skinny that he could hook his feet together without crushing her.

It was about eight kilometres to Hien Gong Huy, and Ah Wei slept for most of the journey. Ah Ngange was hardly out of breath—she had walked everywhere all her life and was used to carrying burdens on her back for long distances. She did not consider her grandson to be a burden.

Ah Thloo walked behind her along the dirt path between the rice fields, carrying the suitcase. As they passed through the fields, the sharp smell of recently spread night soil followed them all the way.

A regularly scheduled bus stopped in the market village to take people to the riverside city of Thlam Fow, where Ah Thloo and her son would board the boat taking them up the river to Guangzhou. Ah Ngange would go back home from there, and when she stopped walking to let Ah Wei down, he started to cry, howling loudly. His little arms, wrapped around her neck, now refused to let go.

"Don't cry, my Gowdoy; you are big now. Your Ah Yea won't like to see you cry. I'll see you soon."

Wrenching his hands apart, Ah Ngange turned him to face her and hugged him fiercely. It was the first time Ah Thloo had seen her mother-in-law cry. Tears seeped out of the corners of her eyes, but before she released the boy, she wiped them from her face, leaving sooty streaks. Straightening up, she opened Ah Thloo's hand and deliberately transferred the small boy's struggling fingers to his mother's strong grasp. Without another word, she turned and headed home.

Ah Thloo felt her own hot tears stream down her cheeks as she attempted to quell the heartache her son was sharing so loudly; it was hard not to empathize with the old woman. Also, she was feeling the anxiety of what was to come.

o · o · o

In Guangzhou, they rented a room in a large house, recommended to them by a neighbour from their hamlet. It was a surprisingly modern home, and Ah Thloo was especially impressed by the conveniences of indoor plumbing. Rather than having to draw water from a well, it came from a tap inside the house. She had used one of these before when she and Ah Dang had come to the city a few years earlier.

Here, though, she saw something truly amazing: an indoor toilet. It consisted of a raised ceramic area on the floor with a hole over which a person squatted. Water from a bucket was ladled over it to flush, and Ah Thloo assumed the waste was collected wherever the drain ended. The landlady just laughed when Ah Thloo asked about it and assured her the drains emptied into the harbour. Imagine a place that no longer required its night soil as fertilizer! She was starting to experience a new world.

The landlady was known simply as Ah Law Ah Hoo, Old Granny. She had jat giek, bound feet. She was a well-to-do widow whose only son and daughter-in-law had died recently, leaving a daughter whom Old Granny was raising on her own. They were a loving pair, each taking care of the other. Ah Thloo was reminded, with heartbreaking clarity, of her own dear Ah Ngange and herself as a young girl.

They quickly all got to know one another and started to share meals. The girl, Ah Ngan Jean, was a few years younger than Ah Lai, and the two girls met when Ah Thloo sent her daughter tickets to come to Guangzhou for a holiday. Ah Lai had just graduated from high school and the trip was to celebrate her hard work and success. Ah Thloo hoped that she and her daughter would use the time for a reconciliation.

Ah Lai stayed for a month; it was her first visit to the city. They had to be careful with money but managed to sample the dim sum at a different restaurant once a week. They ate simply, but Ah Thloo treated the children to an occasional fresh fish, pork, and *haam toy*, pickled vegetables.

The three spent their days exploring the city. At home and in the market town, travellers' choices in transportation were mostly based on human power—feet or occasionally bicycles. In Guangzhou as well, the roads had more bicycles than motor vehicles, but city buses went everywhere. For a few tien, coins, they could ride the bus for miles, gazing out in amazement at the seemingly endless metropolis, totally under cover, sheltered from the weather. Passing the residential areas inland from Whampoa Harbour, they caught glimpses of European architectural influences, in the Western-style mansions of former shipping barons.

It was easy to spend hours at the markets, where they shopped for food every day. The markets were much larger than any they had been to at home. There was so much to see and do—every sense was bombarded by variety and novelty. Ah Wei was easily bored and tired, so mother and daughter took turns to piggyback him during their walks. Ah Thloo saw that Ah Wei loved having his big sister with him and that they doted on each other.

The place they liked best was a park just a few blocks from the house. It was built around a tranquil lake, dotted with fragrant gardens, tall pagodas, and delicately arched bridges. It was very peaceful and they spent a lot of time there. Sometimes they included Ah Ngan Jean and her grandmother on their outings.

One day, Ah Thloo took her daughter shopping to buy a special gradu-ation present with money sent by Ah Dang for this express purpose. They chose a short-sleeved, A-line dress, in a multicoloured flower print. The next day, with her hair tied in ribbons, wearing the dress, embroidered ankle socks, and a new pair of black Mary Jane shoes, Ah Lai had her picture taken. Knowing the photo was for her father, she stood tall and straight, smiled shyly, and looked thoroughly modern. Over the month, Ah Thloo felt she and her daughter had come to an understanding, and they had a warm, though weepy, leave-taking.

While Ah Thloo waited another few months for travel documents, she filled the time by getting to know Ah Ngan Jean. She had developed a soft spot in her heart for the youngster. Ah Ngan Jean was a serious girl, content with life. She was also smart, with a bright future ahead of her, if given the opportunity of an education. Having spent time with Ah Lai, the younger girl was also keen on the idea of schooling.

Old Granny was a traditionalist and had not considered it necessary for the girl to be educated. After meeting Ah Lai, however, she saw that school-ing had not spoiled the girl's manners. Ah Thloo couldn't know how long Old Granny would live, but when she died, Ah Ngan Jean would be left on her own, without anyone to guide or sponsor her. Ah Thloo felt she had to do something. She sought agreement from her husband to contribute to Ah Ngan Jean's education, which helped pursuade the older woman to allow her granddaughter to go to school. Through a pledge, Ah Thloo became the girl's *kai ma*, godmother.

Again, when the time came for their next move, Ah Thloo did not tell her daughter beforehand that they were leaving for Hong Kong, in the British Territories. Ah Lai had to learn from Ah Ngan Jean that her mother and little brother had left the country. No one knew when any of them would ever see one another again.

o o o

Friends in Guangzhou arranged accommodations for Ah Thloo and Ah Wei in Hong Kong, where they had one bed in a small room in a large, crowded apartment building. The cooking area and washing facilities were at the end of a hall, which they shared with families on the same floor. Everything was so cramped that only one person could cook at a time. Mealtimes were

Ah Thloo, Ah Wei, and goddaughter, Ah Ngan Jean, 1952.
UNKNOWN PHOTOGRAPHY STUDIO, CHINA

hectic, as all the women jostled for space, screeching at one another if they didn't get their way. Ah Thloo preferred to wait till everyone was finished. It was easier, even if they had to eat much later.

They were in Hong Kong for almost a year and a half, waiting for Canada's response to their visa application. It was a strange, lonely, and uncertain time—*m'loy, m'heuy*, they weren't coming or going.

Their saving grace came in the form of a young man, Ah Sang, the son of one of Ah Thloo's housemates from the nui oak in her home village, who was waiting for his own travel visa to go to Australia. Ah Thloo was grateful to have a contact in case she needed help but did not expect him to do much. How much attention and time would an eighteen-year-old boy give to an old married woman and a child?

Ah Thloo, Ah Sang, and Ah Wei, 1953.
UNKNOWN PHOTOGRAPHER, HONG KONG

What a surprise it was when Ah Sang showed up at their door one day and asked if they had time to go out. He was like an angel to them during that period and an attentive big brother to Ah Wei. He took them sightseeing several times. One exciting adventure was a trip up to the exclusive lookout at Victoria Peak. Ah Wei clutched his mother's legs and hid his head as they rode the cable tram up the steep hill. The higher they rode, the broader grew the view—of the city, the harbour, and the islands of Lantau and Lamma. Even more stunning were the sprawling mansions perched on the hillside.

"Yes, those are actually houses," Ah Sang confirmed when Ah Thloo asked.

"They live like the old emperors!" It was hard to believe the Chinese Revolution had not extended this far.

They had pictures taken on the promenade. Ah Wei was posed in front of an expensive-looking sedan, smart in his white shirt, short pants, and suspenders. Unfortunately for them, Ah Sang's visa came through in 1953 and he left them to start his new life in Australia. Before he left, he pledged to keep in touch with Ah Thloo, and although they did not formalize their relationship as Ah Thloo had done with Ah Ngan Jean, they acted as if they had, for the rest of their lives.

o   o   o

Throughout this time in limbo, as the bureaucratic wheels advanced one slow cog at a time, Ah Thloo tried to keep busy. In Canada, Ah Dang was reinventing himself again. They kept in touch by mail.

Ah Dang encouraged her to enrol Ah Wei in school; it would give the boy some structure and a head start in learning English. He suggested the English name of "Robert" for his son, in the event the school required one for enrolment.

Ah Thloo found a good school a short bus ride from their apartment. Ah Wei's teacher told her that the boy was an obedient student but got frustrated when he didn't understand a new concept.

Ah Dang sent her two pieces of the best news in December 1953. The first was that the Canadian Immigration Department had approved their applications. He sent her instructions for the next steps in the process: she would have to meet with the superintendent of Canadian Immigration, bringing passport-type photographs, and arrangements would be made for free medical exams, including X-rays. His other news was that he had joined some Chinese friends to run a restaurant. The group had just bought an existing business and was fixing it up to open in the coming year. He noted that one of the partners had a son the same age as Ah Lai and a daughter the same age as Ah Wei; they could all be friends. He wrote, "You are making my dreams come true. First my family will be together. Now I will be a business-man! I hope you and our son will be in Canada in time to help me celebrate the opening."

Ah Thloo wrote back to congratulate him but was sad to report that for some reason, there were to be delays of several months at the Immigration Office. She sent her husband a photo of them at the Peak.

Ah Dang reported on the official opening of the restaurant. The China Garden Café, Ltd., at 1240 Stanley Street, across the square from the Sun Life Building, started business on March 23, 1954. The full-sized window facing the street was filled with congratulatory baskets of bright flowers from surrounding businesses. All day and night, people kept coming in to buy a cup of coffee and have a free almond cookie. Some even stayed for a meal. Ah Dang said they were right not to go to *Hong Ngange gai*, Chinatown, where only Chinese people shopped; the *Thlai Ngange*, Western people, spent more money on eating meals out.

Ah Thloo was happy to hear of his success but also expressed her hope of living in Chinatown, if that was where she could converse with people of her own kind. "What is coffee?" she added.

Ah Dang told her he had found a second-storey walk-up apartment on de Bullion Street, just a short bus ride from Chinatown. He warned her that it was not as spacious as their house in China, but it was all he could afford for now.

Ah Thloo's next news was not good. The Canadian Immigration Office had sent a letter with an appointment for August 24, 1954, requiring Ah Thloo and Ah Wei to show evidence of immunity from smallpox within the last three years, but they had no such papers. She was arranging for vaccinations.

Ah Dang was worried that by the time she came to Canada, the weather would be getting cold and instructed her to purchase the warmest woollen coats she could find. Hoping against hope, he also sent her money to buy airplane tickets.

China Garden Café's grand opening, 1954.
UNKNOWN PHOTOGRAPHER, MONTREAL

On November 22, 1954, Ah Thloo, with the family name of Wong (née Jang), and her given names anglicized as Tue Sue, and Ah Wei, renamed Robert Yuet Wei Wong, were approved to go to Canada. At long last.

o o o

AH THLOO: ALASKA, DECEMBER 24, 1954

Ah Thloo had had many firsts along the journey thus far; the airplane ride literally launched her into the twentieth century. The flight stopped in Alaska, where the plane was refuelled after all the passengers had disembarked. Ah Thloo had looked forward to getting out of the stuffy plane, and breathing some fresh air, but when it landed and she looked out the window, everything was covered in white. Ah Dang had told her about snow, but until that moment, she had not really believed that it could blanket the world. When she and Ah Wei stepped out the door, he laughed at what he thought was smoke coming out of her nostrils, but it was just her breath. He was surprised and delighted to see it coming out of his nose and mouth too.

Their hot meal was loaded in Alaska, and they were served dinner as soon as the plane had reached its cruising altitude. Ah Thloo did not realize they had just tasted their first Christmas turkey dinner. Neither did she understand, at the time, the significance of the date of her arrival, December 24. In the Christian calendar, she later learned, Christmas is a celebration of the birth of hope.

Reunited at last with his family (a part of it, at least), this was the best present Ah Dang could have received. They all posed among his friends in Montreal's Dorval Airport. In one hand, Ah Dang held his fedora, while the other clasped his young son's arm. As he looked down at the boy, a grin of happiness and pride lit up his face. His days of being a part-time husband had ended. Even better, he was now the full-time father of his son.

Ah Wei, the object of his father's attention, was solemn. His big, round eyes looked directly at the camera. The six-year-old looked like a little gentleman in his modern suit, but the impression was offset by the jauntily worn Santa cap on his head.

Ah Thloo stood behind the boy, also looking quite modern with her head of short, carefully permed hair, her expression enigmatic.

Reunited at Dorval Airport in 1954. Back, left to right: Mrs. J. Tang
(wife of Ah Dang's business partner), Ah Thloo, Miss Susan Mah
(who flew with Ah Thloo), and a family friend named Lewis.
Front, left to right: P. Tang, Ah Wei, and Ah Dang.

JASPER TANG, MONTREAL

Aye, bee, see, dee, ee, ef-fu, jee—these letters aren't too hard to learn, thought Ah Thloo, *but others are so difficult to pronounce! Something about rolling the tongue, or blowing air through the teeth, but when I try those things, the sounds never come out the same way. Like the letter "F"—the beginning "eh" sound is easy, but how do you blow air for the "fu" without making a sound? Aiya, what a hard language! But I have to keep practising; can't always rely on the children to speak for me.*

ELEVEN

Father Rejuvenated, Mother Baptized

AH THLOO: MONTREAL, 1965

It was late on a winter afternoon, and Ah Dang and Ah Thloo were shopping downtown for Christmas presents. It would take them more than an hour to get home, so he said to his wife, "You must be hungry. Let's go have something to eat." She thought, *Dinner out. What a pleasant treat!*

Ah Dang had very pedestrian tastes in food. He ate like a Canadian teenager: Kraft peanut butter and orange marmalade on whole wheat bread, Velveeta cheese, kosher all-beef frankfurters, and applesauce. Every day, at home or at work, he drank either Red Rose or Po-Neh tea. If he was at home for an "offu day," which is how the family referred to his day off work, he would bake an apple pie or roast a joint of beef. Unless it was at a banquet, he rarely ate in Chinatown. He used to say he was tired of eating restaurant food.

A typical "offu day" with the children, playing at
the War Memorial on Park Avenue, 1956.
T.S. WONG, MONTREAL

On the shopping afternoon, he took his wife to a restaurant on St.
Catherine Street. He ordered coffee and a muffin for himself and asked her
what she wanted. She could not read the menu and had no idea what to order.
Shocked and disappointed, all she could murmur was, "I'm not hungry."

o o o

AH THLOO AND AH DANG: MONTREAL, 1955–1966

Ah Thloo and Ah Dang were celebrating their first Chinese New Year
together when their third and last child was conceived. It was a surprise, for
she was forty-four and he was fifty-three, ages when most of their predeces-
sors had become grandparents.

For the first time, both the pregnancy and the birth were hard on Ah Thloo.
She had to give birth in a hospital: she was weak and produced no milk. Their
daughter was born on October 12, 1955. The hospital required that a name for
the child be recorded on a birth certificate before the mother and baby could
be released to go home. It was disconcerting for the parents, as they would

A pregnant Ah Thloo at the Botanical Gardens with Ah Wei, 1955.
GD WONG, MONTREAL

normally have waited for the one-month Choot Ngiet Gat How ceremony to announce a name. But these were the Canadian customs.

Like her sister before her, the baby was given the middle name of Quen. Her first name was May, meaning "beautiful." Coincidentally, the word "may" in Chinese also sounds like the word for "final" or "last."

A month after the baby was brought home, Ah Dang wrote to inform his mother and parents-in-law about the birth of another granddaughter and enclosed money for celebratory feasts. Despite Ah Thloo's inability to breast-feed the baby, and their initial fears for its health, the child thrived, first on formula, then on cow's milk. Ah Dang reported that the baby was fat and active when presented to their friends, on the occasion of her one-month haircutting event.

Ah Tew May wrote back to say she was glad her Gowdoy, as she always referred to her grandson, Ah Wei, had a new playmate. Ah Shee, Ah Thloo's mother, then aged seventy-five, wrote on behalf of Ah Poy Lim, seventy-eight, and herself, sending polite congratulations to their son-in-law and daughter. Three years later, Ah Shee would be dead, and her husband would be living as a hermit in a hut away from the village, visiting his former home only to get food. He died in 1960, at the age of eighty-three, a once proud and capable man, overcome by the unrelenting social, economic, and political upheavals of his times.

Christmas at Bagg Street, 1959.
ROBERT WONG, MONTREAL

The younger generation, when informed by Ah Thloo, responded with enthusiasm about the baby and with concerned inquiries about her health. If her daughter Ah Lai, goddaughter Ah Ngan Jean, or godson Ah Sang were surprised, no one mentioned it, and each sent a small gift along with good wishes. Not too long afterwards, Ah Lai started her own family.

Ah May's birth rejuvenated Ah Dang. He gave her a twenty-four-carat gold charm bracelet, hung with delicately tinkling bells and small animals at her one-month ceremony, to welcome her. He now had the chance to witness a child of his grow from infancy to school age and adulthood. At first, whenever he got home from work late at night, he would relax by smoking and watching her as she slept. When she coughed each time he lit a cigarette, he stopped, "cold turkey," a pack-a-day habit he had started more than thirty years earlier. As she grew, his hands would search for hers to hold whenever they went out. He was making up for lost time, when there was no family member he could touch and cherish. He recorded the lives of his two younger children on his camera and, later, in movies.

Shortly after the birth of his daughter, Ah Dang bought a three-storey residential building on Bagg Street, a short side street off St. Laurent Boulevard, in an area of Montreal known as The Main. Since they had come to Canada, the Wong family had been living in rented rooms on de Bullion Street, but when Ah Thloo mentioned that rats had brushed her feet, scurrying around the bedroom while she fed the baby at night, it was enough to spur Ah Dang to find another place.

The house cost fourteen thousand dollars; he paid half down and got a mortgage from the vendor, Myer Patofsky, a tailor, at 6 per cent interest for the remainder, until 1972. It was thirty-four years to the month after he had landed in Vancouver, four years since he had become a citizen, and only a year since he had been elevated from a mere waiter to a restaurant keeper. Now he was a home owner!

No other Chinese lived on the street. The neighbours were older European immigrants, mostly Jewish, from Poland or Hungary, probably Holocaust survivors. Everyone there wanted to be Canadian, but nobody quite knew how; the children ate what their parents cooked—food from their countries of origin—and at home they spoke the language of their parents' parents. Few of them spoke English. Ah Thloo did not go out to socialize with the neighbours, except to greet the elderly ones on either side of her, who always said, "Hello!" as she passed. They wouldn't let her refuse their gifts of candies and cookies, and took every chance to pat Ah Wei's and Ah May's heads.

Only a few of the families had children, and all of them somehow learned to speak English, even without any native English speaker around. Ah May played with the girls who lived on the street while Ah Wei spent time with the neighbourhood boys he knew from school, but everyone was kept indoors after dusk.

All the parents kept a close eye on the children; they never went into one another's houses. If Ah Wei or Ah May happened to be on a neighbour's front stoop at mealtime, Ah Thloo would call out, "*Ah We-iii, Ah Maa-ay,* come home and eat." Her children were expected to drop whatever they were doing and leave immediately. If they did not, she would just keep on calling. In that neighbourhood, everyone's mother yelled out. Across the street,

Muscha's mother, an anxious Hungarian, would call out her daughter's name every hour. They lived on the second floor and had a bird's-eye view of the street, so Muscha just had to stand up to be seen and assure her mother she hadn't been taken away.

The house on Bagg Street was a typical Montreal triplex, with a wooden staircase leading to a balcony on the second floor. One door off the balcony led to the second-storey apartment, while another opened to a flight of indoor stairs to the third-floor apartment. The Wongs lived on the ground floor, number 74 and leased the two upstairs apartments, mostly to Chinese families related to them in some way.

This house had rats as well, but the rodents stayed behind the walls and under the floorboards. Each evening, the family heard them scratching and scurrying from one end of the building to the other. A trapdoor in the floor of the bathroom opened into a crawl space under the house where Ah Dang, and later Ah Wei, laid rat traps baited with smelly Swiss cheese.

Ah Thloo and Ah May shared the front bedroom on one side of the main entrance hall. They slept in twin beds, facing a window that looked out to the front garden, where Ah Thloo planted vegetables. Ah Dang had a double bed in the adjoining room. There was no wall between the rooms, but a plastered crossbeam on the ceiling separated the spaces.

Ah Wei had his own room down the hall, off the living room. He had a view of the backyard—really just a dirt patch where not even dandelions grew. The three balconies faced onto the back. A sweet Jewish widow lived on the second floor of the house across from the Wongs. She used to throw down bags of candy and tried to engage Ah Thloo in conversation; Ah Thloo would eventually smile back, wave, and say, "Hello, howyu?"

The room across the hall from the front bedroom was Ah Thloo's refuge. It stored all the precious things she had brought from China. It was also her workroom, where she could sew household items and clothes for herself and the children on a black Singer treadle machine.

One half of the room was lined with jars and tin boxes filled with traditional Chinese ingredients for health, long life, and vitality. Ah Thloo could have stocked an herbalist's shop. There were gallon-sized Mason jars that held whole snakes pickled in brandy to fortify it for its vitalizing effects; she would ladle a small cup for the adults to sip at Chinese New Year. She also made rice wine, letting it ferment in the jars; it exuded a sour, bitter smell whenever the lid was opened. Again, the wine was drunk only on special occasions.

Enclosed in individual, large, airtight tin boxes were dried abalone, sea cucumber, seahorses, shrimp, sharks' fins, scallops, seaweed, and sea grass. There were also dried mushrooms, lily stalks, wood ear fungus, herbs, dates, red goji berries, ginseng roots, hard round teacakes, and clusters of birds' nests. Every day, she would make delicious soups using some of these ingredients. Others were reserved for special occasions. *Yen waw gaang*, birds' nest soup, and *nguey chee gaang*, sharks' fin soup, were favourite dishes eaten during New Year celebrations or birthdays.

The largest item in the room was a deep blue, metal travel trunk with brass bands and studs, which Ah Thloo had brought from Hong Kong. In it was a silk-covered comforter, stuffed with cotton, used only on very cold nights. It was fuchsia-pink on one side and turquoise on the other. The inside of the trunk, lined in blue silk, had an enduring fragrance from the bags of dried cinnamon sticks stored there.

Besides the traditional Chinese medicines, Ah Thloo had brought with her many of the traditional ways of preserving foods, one of which was to use the hot Montreal summer temperatures to cure food outdoors. Ah Dang made a special pressing rack, as well as a drying box, from wood lined with chicken wire and metal mesh to keep out flies. The door swung out and was secured with a wooden dowel and extra wire. The box was hung from a hook out on the back balcony.

After marinating strips of fatty pork belly in a mixture of gin, spices, sugar, and soy sauce, Ah Thloo strung the meat on a cotton string, using a large darning needle, and hung it in the box. This cured pork belly was called *lap ngoke*, and a small piece was all that was needed to add rich flavour to a dish. Sometimes she hung a whole marinated duck that had been split in half and pressed flat in the homemade rack. *Lap ap*, the cured duck, was a delicacy that made Ah Dang's mouth water just thinking about it.

The European neighbours, especially the nice Jewish lady across the backyard, were very interested in the processes and were always asking Ah Thloo what was in the box. However, being wary, she would feign ignorance, shrug her shoulders, and smile blandly before retreating into the house.

Ah Thloo shopped for groceries every few days. She received a portion of Ah Dang's weekly pay and managed the household from her own bank account. Although she had a refrigerator, all Chinese like to eat fresh foods, and shopping was a good excuse to get out of the house. She had a number of expandable string bags to carry the groceries. Until Ah May joined Ah Wei at Devonshire Elementary School, she accompanied Ah Thloo everywhere.

The Warshaw Grocery on St. Laurent, where Ah Thloo bought fruit, vegetables, and staples, was only two blocks from the house. Rice and Chinese vegetables like bok choy and gai lan could then be found only in Chinatown, where the family went every weekend.

Meat was selected from the Hungarian butcher shop a few doors down the street, where the clean smell of fresh sawdust was a counterpoint to the metallic odour of blood and the aromas of various spices. Ah Thloo might buy a piece of pork, cut from a leg displayed in the cooler. The meat was wrapped in a sheet of pink paper that was waxed on the inside and tied with a piece of string.

Processed meats were sold on the other side of the store. Tubes of round sausages were displayed behind the counter: long, short, thick, thin, fatty, dry, dark, light, all suspended from a railing hung from the ceiling. The salty, spicy, savoury smells from that side of the store always tantalized Ah May's nose and tastebuds, but Ah Thloo, unfamiliar with the food, and being frugal, never bought any.

On the counters were displays of silk stockings (the kind that were held up by a garter belt) and fine hairnets in various colours. There were European confections, hard fruit candies with liquid centres, brightly coloured marzipan that was shaped into fruits or animals, and black liquorice drops.

The next stop was on Roy Street, where Waldman's Fish Store and Liebovich Poultry were located. At the time, Waldman's was just a cold warehouse filled with tanks of fish and shellfish such as lobsters, crabs, and prawns. Rows of trays on long tables held different varieties of fresh fish, covered in chipped ice. Some still twitched, their mouths kissing the air, seeking water. The floors ran with water and scales and occasionally blood and guts. Ah Thloo walked around the tables, poking eyes with a bare finger and lifting gills to see how fresh the fish were. The chosen fish was wrapped in newspaper.

If the fish were deemed unworthy, Ah Thloo took Ah May to Liebovich Poultry, referred to as Lie Giek Doy, Crippled Boy's. This store was a small space filled with old, dirty metal cages, stuffed with chickens of all shapes, colours, ages, and sizes. There were ducks, pigeons, and turkeys as well. The birds' body heat increased the temperature and enhanced the smell of the cramped, steamy room. The aroma was a mixture of chicken droppings, warm blood, and faintly fishy, faintly burnt feathers. Ah Thloo chose not to pay the extra charge for slaughtering, so with its wings trussed and feet tied together, the clucking chicken was stuffed into a string bag.

Loaded with the makings of a meal, mother and daughter walked home. Once Ah Dang was awake, Ah Thloo went about dispatching the chicken, always a noisy job, as the chicken inevitably squawked. However, she was efficient and sure-handed with her sharp, wooden-handled cleaver, chopping the head off in a single blow.

Whatever foods Ah Thloo could not make, she bought in Chinatown. Leong Jung, at 92 De La Gauchetière West, was a favourite grocery store. A gentle-spoken, white-haired man called Ah Lee Bak and his two sons owned it. Ah Thloo's family was always welcomed with a cup of tea, poured from an oversized ceramic pot that was kept warm in a woven and lined tea cozy. The adults would exchange news and Chinatown gossip, while Ah May wandered through the aisles.

On the floor were rows of open burlap bags overflowing with exotic-smelling herbs and spices, square metal buckets of fresh tofu swimming in water, and rectangular wooden boxes of fresh garden vegetables. On shelves along the walls were stacked large tins of preserved vegetables, meats or fish, and sauces, as well as earthen jars filled with pungent salted black beans or thick molasses. In the back corner of the store, suspended on a black hook a foot long, in a frame that looked like an upended metal coffin, hung a whole roasted pig, smelling deliciously of a special blend of spices. As the day wore on, chunks would be cut from its carcass—the most desirable parts from its savoury ribs, topped with a coat of crispy, light, crackled skin. Ah Thloo splurged on a piece of the savoury pork from time to time. From the ceiling were hung cured meats and strings of the store's famous homemade *lap cheong*, Chinese sausages. They had several varieties, including, duck, chicken, pork, and even one that was like a blood sausage. At home, Ah Thloo would cut a sausage into chunks and steam them on top of rice, the rich, sweet flavour and oil permeating the whole pot. Having arrived from China with recent memories of starvation, she at first enjoyed the fatty bits. Later, when she was more health conscious, she meticulously excavated each piece of hard white fat before cooking the meat.

Occasionally, she shopped downtown, travelling everywhere by bus, making use of Montreal's efficient transit system. A single, inexpensive fare could take her all the way across the island, transferring from one bus to another. During the ride, Ah Thloo stayed vigilant, taking note of landmarks so she could remember the way home. She shopped mostly in the department stores on St. Catherine Street. Henry Morgan's Store and Eaton's, where they had a "no questions asked" refund policy, were her favourites.

Although Ah Thloo took some English lessons at the Chinese Presbyterian Church, she learned much of her English from watching television and late-night movies. Ah Dang bought a small, black-and-white television set with rabbit-ear antennae. During the day, *Howdy Doody* was on, and in the evenings, Ah Thloo and the two children watched shows such as *Red Skelton, I Love Lucy*, and *Ed Sullivan*. Ah Thloo learned to laugh with the televised laugh track. Late at night, she watched movies, accompanied by Ah Wei on the weekends, after Ah May had gone to bed. Ah Thloo never let on how much she actually understood of the English dialogue, preferring to speak to the children in Chinese.

o   o   o

The year 1955 was the start of a rewarding time for Ah Dang. In addition to the birth of his daughter, he was becoming successful in his relatively new career as a businessman. For work, he groomed himself carefully. His nails were neatly trimmed and clean. He brushed his hair and added a fragrant pomade to hold it in place. He wore formal dress socks, sometimes held up with garters, and kept his leather shoes polished to a hard shine. On the way to work, he always wore a fedora, which changed with the seasons—a felt one in the winter and straw in the summer. He always wore a suit, usually grey, with a white shirt and tie, sometimes a bow tie.

At the restaurant, Ah Dang replaced his suit jacket with a white cotton jacket, trimmed in maroon, to distinguish him from the waiters, who had jackets with green accents. He worked the till at the front of the restaurant and helped serve when required, but unless he mentioned it, few customers would have known he had a stake in the business.

Bagg Street house (boarded up after a fire). It has since been restored, 2004.

MAY Q. WONG, MONTREAL

Ah Dang with two of China Garden's wait staff
(standing on right is Ah Chiang Hoo's son).
UNKNOWN PHOTOGRAPHER, MONTREAL

The China Garden Café was located in the heart of Montreal's shopping
and business area and served Chinese-Canadian food to a varied clientele.
Facing Dominion Square, it was a popular lunch spot for downtown office
workers and shoppers. An ad published in the October 10, 1958, issue of
the *Canadian Jewish Review* claimed the restaurant was "very convenient
for ladies to meet their friends while shopping." At night, clients came from
surrounding establishments, such as the elegant Windsor Hotel, for a quick
bite before catching a movie or for a more leisurely meal after a cabaret show.
The restaurant could also be booked for parties.

The front part of the establishment was set up with large booths that could seat six people comfortably. On the wall in each booth was a small jukebox that played the latest North American hit songs. There was a dining room in the back, which could accommodate fifty to seventy people. The banquet menu had such items as *war siew guy*, stuffed crispy chicken. This was a rich and time-consuming dish to make, served on special occasions. It recreated a chicken, with a meat mixture that was stuffed into a whole chicken skin, then deep-fried. Ah Dang sometimes took one home for the family's New Year's dinner party. The restaurant also made the city's best egg rolls and almond cookies.

The kitchen was on the ground floor at the back of the restaurant, where it opened onto a back alley and a private parking lot. The floors were raised on a wooden platform, and two gas ranges held four or five large woks each. A set of stairs led down to the basement, to the refrigerators, coolers, and preparation room. That was also where the office was located and where the resident mousers lived. The cool dimness of the underground room was a haven in the hot, humid summers.

The noise, from the waiters shouting orders, the whoosh of the gas flames, the clanging of metal spatulas flipping food in the metal woks, the hiss of wet fresh vegetables in hot oil, the *bock*! of a sharp cleaver on wooden chopping blocks, and the shouts of cooks calling up plates of steaming hot food was a show in itself, but Montreal had more than enough entertainment.

The restaurant was a few doors from a strip club and a number of jazz bars. By the mid-1950s, the city was at the tail end of its heyday in the Golden Era of music as *the* place to be for the likes of Peggy Lee, Oscar Peterson, and Frank Sinatra. Montreal was becoming known as Sin City, its bars, brothels, and strip clubs run by gangsters. Open twenty-four hours a day, the China Garden was a favourite place for midnight snacks or late-night munchies between sets. Many of the clients were Americans who thought they were immune to Canadian laws, but Ah Dang proved them wrong. He worked the night shift and saw the worst of the offenders.

Ah Dang looked innocuous enough in his work clothes, but he was the enforcer in the restaurant. Every few weeks, he would get home late because someone had tried, unsuccessfully, to eat and run—literally, without paying for his meal. But Ah Dang would not let the culprit leave. He owned two items not normally packed by a restaurateur—a knuckle-duster and a leather sap, which he had learned to use effectively many years earlier.

Only five feet four inches tall, with arms akimbo, holding his sap, eyes bulging with indignation, he could look fierce, like a raging pit bull terrier. He worked too hard to let anyone take advantage of him by not paying. He would block the front door and tell his colleagues in the back to call the police. Sometimes there were scuffles and he was hurt, but never seriously; he still remembered how to protect himself.

The restaurant treated the local beat cops well, giving them free hot coffee and perhaps a meal or two; they always responded quickly. Ah Dang pressed charges when they arrived, which meant he had to go to small claims court the next morning, and this made for a long day. Although he was one of the owners, he never took an extra afternoon or evening off to make up for the court time. He did it all to be sure he got justice.

In the mornings, he came home around the time that most other fathers would be having breakfast or leaving for work. Ah May was always at the door to greet him. Quickly bussing his scruffy cheek, she would wrap her arms around his neck for a tight hug that was the high point of his day, and he would think, *It's all worth the effort—just for this!*

o   o   o

Just as Ah Dang was helped by his adoptive father and Ah Ngay Gonge to settle in Canada, he in turn assisted others. Many people were given a hand to adjust; some were even related.

A number of single women stayed with the family before they got married. One young woman who maintained close ties was Ma Toy Yee, Ah Thloo's eldest sister's daughter. Ah Yee came to Montreal from Hong Kong in 1960, as a bride to Wong Chuck Min (distantly related to Ah Dang), who worked as a cook at China Garden. At twenty-two, Ah Yee was vivacious, glamorous, and great fun, and Ah May, then only five, thought she was her big sister.

The family accompanied the newlyweds on their honeymoon to Niagara Falls, because Ah Dang had to interpret for them; neither of them spoke any English at the time. When each of their first three children was born, it was Ah Dang who took his niece to the hospital and awaited the birth, and it was Ah Thloo who taught her niece how to bathe, change, and feed her first baby.

Back, left to right: Ah Thloo, Ah Min, and Ah Wei.
Front, left to right: Anna, Ah Yee with Helen, and Truman, *circa* 1960s.
MAY Q. WONG, MONTREAL

By the time their fourth and last child was born, Ah Min was able to accompany his wife on his own. At first the couple shared an apartment with Ah Min's elder brother, but the growing family needed more room, and they moved to the third-floor apartment on Bagg Street as soon as it was available. Ah Thloo and Ah Dang were surrogate grandparents for the children, a wellspring of wisdom, toys, and adventures.

Although Ah Dang had moved away from Chinatown, he never forgot those who had stayed behind. He and Ah Thloo regularly took Ah Wei and Ah May to visit different Ah Baks, Elder Uncles, who may or may not have been actually related.

Mostly, they lived in dark rooming houses above the stores that lined Chinatown, with rickety, dark stairways leading to rooms resembling rabbit warrens, but with less air. The men shared cooking, cleaning, and bathroom facilities. Each had a small personal space, enough for a single bed, a chair, a dresser, a small table, and shelves to hold non-perishable foods, a book or two, and perhaps some photographs. The rooms weren't always totally contained; sometimes there were only half-walls on either side, with a cloth curtain drawn across the front of the cubicle for privacy. The men could hear their neighbours snoring, coughing, talking to visitors, snapping a newspaper, or listening to the radio. The place smelled of stale sweat, unwashed bodies, and cigarette smoke. Always, they lived alone. Their wives and families, if they had any, were in China.

A part of Chinese etiquette was to bring *siu thlem*, a small gift, whenever one visited another person's home. Usually, it was oranges. When the Wong family visited the Ah Baks, they would bring a little more, perhaps a piece of *char sui*, Chinese barbequed pork, or half a roast chicken, for the men's meals that evening. Ah Dang also brought them packages of tobacco and cigarette paper.

The men made a fuss over the children, marvelling at how big they were and telling them to be studious, and to *hiang wa*, listen to being told, be obedient. They missed being able to tell their own children these universal lessons.

One very old Ah Bak lived in a laundry on St. Hubert Street, close to the city's downtown area. Ah Dang always brought extra gifts whenever the family went to visit, which was about every three months. In a large paper bag, Ah May would see her father pack a bottle of whisky, a dozen oranges, a string of Chinese sausages, a large tin of tobacco, and a variety of cooked meats from Chinatown that would have fed their own family for a week. It wasn't until decades later that she figured out he was *the* Ah Ngay Gonge who had helped her father come to Montreal.

Nor did Ah Thloo or Ah Dang forget the families they had left behind in China. Ah Dang sent money to Ah Lai and his mother. Ah Thloo's Christian instruction taught her that forgiveness was right, and she had forgiven her mother, her brother, and his wife for the time during the war with Japan, when they had turned their backs on her. She understood that they had made a mistake in judgment then—desperate times had made them do it.

She taught her children filial duty by supporting her family. Faithfully, every month, Ah Thloo sent a portion of the money she had set aside from Ah Dang's weekly pay to purchase a bank draft from the Nanyang Commercial Bank in Hong Kong, with instructions for the dispersal of funds to her parents and other relatives. While the amounts were diminished after the deaths of her parents, she sent money to China each spring for Qing Ming, Grave Sweeping Day.

Ah Thloo did not adhere to the traditional Chinese attitudes toward boys and girls in families. She had always considered her younger brother as part of her family, just as her married daughter was still counted as *her* daughter. Blood was a stronger tie than tradition. Blood transcended lapses in judgment.

o   o   o

In August 1961, Ah Lai married her high school sweetheart, Guan Haw One, following the new conventions of the People's Republic of China. Wearing similarly plain outfits consisting of a new, homemade, button-down blouse for her and shirt for him, dark pants, and sturdy leather shoes, the couple was joined in matrimony before a government registrar. Again, following the new custom of equality between the sexes and recognizing that women were no longer chattels, Ah Lai signed the certificate using her own family name—Wong Lai Quen. It was not until a month later, after she had completed her studies, that the couple could travel back to their home villages to celebrate with Ah Ngange and her husband's mother. At their respective homes, the couple made obeisance at the family shrines, and feasts were held, to which all the neighbours were invited. Some old conventions were hard to break. Ah Lai's and Ah One's first daughter was born on April 20, 1963.

In Montreal, on April 21, 1963, Ah Thloo and her two younger children were baptized by Reverend Paul Chan and officially inducted into the Chinese Presbyterian Church. "Isn't it funny, we used to worship inanimate things, like rocks and the tombs of ancestors!" said Ah Thloo. Although she never lost her fascination with rocks and natural things, she no longer believed they harboured spirits or represented gods. Instead, she saw God's hand in their creation. And while she continued to send money to China for Ching Ming, to keep the grave markers from being swallowed by the surrounding

Ah Lai and Ah One's engagement photo, 1960.
PHOTOGRAPHER'S STUDIO, CHINA

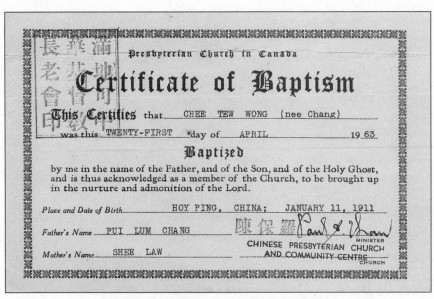

Presbyterian Church in Canada

Certificate of Baptism

This Certifies that ___CHEE TEW WONG___ (nee Chang)

was this ___TWENTY-FIRST___ day of ___APRIL___ 19 63

Baptized

by me in the name of the Father, and of the Son, and of the Holy Ghost, and is thus acknowledged as a member of the Church, to be brought up in the nurture and admonition of the Lord.

Place and Date of Birth ___HOY PING, CHINA; JANUARY 11, 1911___

Father's Name ___PUI LUM CHANG___   陳保羅 Paul S. Chan

                                                    MINISTER

Mother's Name ___SHEE LAW___   CHINESE PRESBYTERIAN CHURCH
                                   AND COMMUNITY CENTRE
                                                    CHURCH

Ah Thloo's baptism certificate—the minister
used his own phonetic translation of her name.

Guey Dang Wong's and Tue Sue Wong's citizenship certificates.

vegetation, she did so as a gesture of respect for her elders, rather than as ancestor worship. After her baptism, she no longer bought and burned incense in the house. "The Church teaches us about Jesus, who died but now lives again. He is a living God. I didn't know any better—no wonder I was so miserable before I converted." Her faith helped her learn to forgive her parents, but she was still learning how to deal with her husband.

Ah Dang was baptized into the United Church of Canada, but on March 28, 1965, he transferred to the congregation of the Chinese Presbyterian Church. He was not a particularly religious man; he hardly ever attended church services. Nevertheless, the church became the family's spiritual and cultural centre. The children attended Chinese School on weekends and church services on Sundays. Between 1965 and 1986, Ah Thloo worked with, and later supervised, the ladies of the Women's Missionary Society, cooking for the annual tea and bazaar fundraiser.

In August 1963, Ah Dang bought 12014 St. Evariste Street, a two-storey duplex with an unfinished basement and underground garage, for twenty-two thousand dollars, half down. The remainder was mortgaged at 7.5 per cent till June 1, 1965. He had decided it was time to move to a newer part of town, but he hadn't consulted much with Ah Thloo.

The new duplex, in the French-Canadian suburb of Cartierville, was just one example of Ah Dang's lack of communication. He had chosen it because of the fresh air and sunshine in the open fields behind the house, and because moving to the suburbs was a mark of upward mobility. One of their fellow church members and his family lived across the street. However, the liveable space in the duplex was smaller than the house on Bagg Street, and it was far away from the shopping and cultural areas frequented by Ah Thloo. As always, she adjusted.

Before Ah Thloo came to Canada, she had thought her time here would be short. Her intention had been to deliver Ah Wei to his father and return to China when the boy became more independent. However, her plans were unexpectedly changed by the birth of their last child. Now that she was to be in the country for a bit longer, she hoped Ah Dang would discuss matters with her before making major decisions, but hope needs to be translated into communication, understanding, acquiescence, and action. All of these take practice. Their wedding night had sown a seed of ill will, and Ah Dang's two subsequent short visits, limited as they were by the threats of war in China and the fear of expulsion from Canada, had not allowed the couple the opportunity to learn how to talk with, or listen to, each other, or to work together as a unit. Certainly, Canada's exclusionary laws, which did not allow Ah Thloo to join her husband, had not helped their situation, forcing them to become independent of each other and to be self-sufficient. Misunderstanding and recrimination were too firmly etched in their relationship to be changed in their middle years.

[Wipe out the] Four Olds—old ideas, old culture, old customs, old habits.

—John King Fairbank, *China: A New History*

TWELVE
Dining with Premier Zhou Enlai

AH MAY: GUANGZHOU, 1966

Black smoke curled up from the wood-burning cookstove, choking Ah Wei and Ah May. The girl was trying, without much effect, to waft the acrid fumes out the narrow door of their uncle's small communal kitchen with sheets of smudged, yellowed newspaper. Their mother was standing outside, keeping a lookout for the other tenants of the building who shared the cooking facility. For the past few days, since their arrival from Canada, they had been the target of the neighbours' unabashed and blatant curiosity; they were *wah kiew*, overseas Chinese, from Ga-na-aie.

The nasty smell and thick smoke were bound to draw someone's attention, and Ah Wei and Ah May needed to complete their work and discard the evidence in secrecy. Ah Thloo's job was to reassure anyone who came and distract them away from the kitchen. Ah May caught snatches of the prayers her mother was murmuring as she paced back and forth in front of the door.

"Dear God, protect us from discovery. Close their prying eyes. Confound their curious ears. Stuff their nosey nostrils."

Ah Wei was supervising the operation. He loved playing with fire, but this was different from any other burn he had conducted. He manoeuvred the object carefully and meticulously over the flames with a pair of old iron tongs.

161

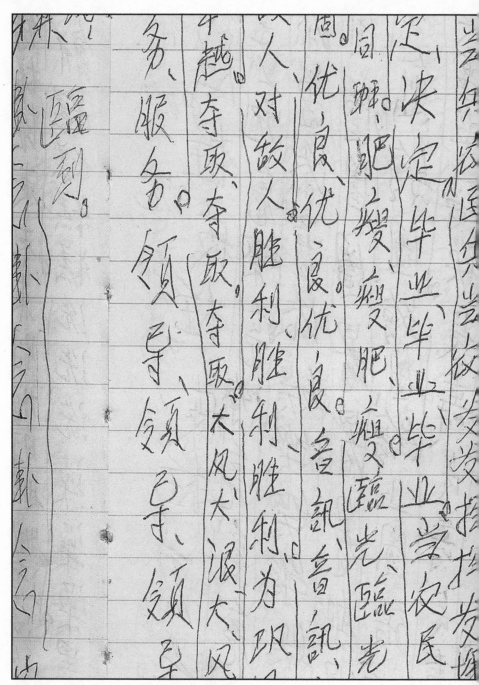

A page from Ah Thloo's homemade Chinese dictionary.

重、严重、严重、困难、困难、困难。

佳美、巧妙、巧妙、巧妙、细致、细致、细致、细

艳色、窗户、艺色、锐利、锐利、座席、座席、疏生

陪伴、陪伴、陪伴、陪伴、座席、座席、正疏生

想见想、大褴、短褴、褴、旗袍、旗袍、旗袍

连连蹉蹉、程度、程度、程度、程度、

创造改变、改变、改变、改变、坚持坚

劳动劳动无锡、无锡、无锡、无锡、

技术技术、棉丝丝棉丝棉邮局邮局

蔬菜。发发发、全高全分

His face, covered in black soot, was streaked with tears from the noxious fumes. Tears streamed down ten-year-old Ah May's face as well, but hers were full of sorrow and loss. With each sizzle, crackle, and ooze, she was losing her one solid connection to the country of her birth, where their father waited for them.

o   o   o

AH DANG: MONTREAL, 1966

"They are more Canadian than Chinese!" said Ah Dang, more and more often, with increasing distress.

While he was proud of his younger children's ability to navigate the Canadian world with their fluent, unaccented English, he did not want them to lose their Chinese heritage. He and Ah Thloo were afraid Ah Wei and Ah May would forget the sacrifices they, and the family in China, had made for the children to live in Canada.

Whenever a letter came from Ah Lai in China, Ah Thloo sat her son and daughter down before reading it out loud. She would sob after reading each sentence to herself before translating the formal, tear-stained phrases into simpler words for the children. It was a long process and difficult for Ah Dang to witness. It made the children uncomfortable too—sometimes he caught them looking at each other over their mother's bowed head, rolling their eyes or sighing with impatience. He had no choice then but to intervene and remind them to listen carefully and to be respectful; these were the words of their Ga Dea, Home Elder Sister.

Ah Dang knew Ah Thloo cried each time she wrote to Ah Lai. Their church had ties to missionary workers in Asia who reported on the dangers in Communist China. His wife thought the worst, and she often blamed him for the forced separation. It was no use arguing that point—he just bit his tongue and retreated behind his newspaper.

It took Ah Thloo many days to write a single letter, first on a sheet of regular lined paper, where words or whole sentences could be crossed out. She had a homemade dictionary, compiled of words and phrases from the newspaper or from their daughter's eloquent letters, and she referred to it often. Ah Dang had once looked through it to find a word but had given up in frustration; it was just a jumble. There was no rhyme or reason to the book's organization—not by origin, sound, or number of strokes. Letter writing was tedious work, but for his wife, it was a labour of pure love. After she had completed the draft, she copied the carefully chosen characters onto a blue airmail form, crying anew. The pale blue, self-sealing airmail form, made of very fine paper, would be blotched and crinkled with tears before it left the house.

Although both parents insisted the children speak Chinese to *them*, neither Ah Wei nor Ah May had progressed much in learning to read and write the language. Despite their attendance at Chinese School every weekend at the church, the children could not recognize even a handful of words from their sister's letters. It was no wonder—they always spoke English to each other. They even had the audacity to call each other by their English names of Robert and May, rather than by the appropriate honorific of Ah Goo, Elder Brother and Ah Moy, Younger Sister. Ah Dang was losing control of them, and he did not understand how that had happened.

Ah Dang had had such high hopes when his family first came to Canada. He had planned to be a *real* father to his son. Ah Gay Sieng, his own adoptive father, had been denied the opportunity, having lived away from home for so long. Then when father and son were finally reunited in Canada, Ah Gay Sieng was struck down by illness and they were separated yet again. Ah Dang had planned to spend time with his own boy, watching him grow, teaching him the ways of a man. But the early years in the restaurant had been harder than he expected, and there was never enough time to spend at home. Now the boy was almost grown and he felt like a stranger.

Ah Thloo told him Ah Wei was staying out at night with his friends. Their neighbour's son, Ah Wei's best friend, had a level head, but Ah Dang did not know anyone else in the group. He knew about being a boy; he could be up to anything.

Ah Wei was apparently interested only in comic books and loud American music—what a waste of money. Ah Dang heard enough of that nonsense at work. He should be able to expect peace and quiet in his own home, but the boy was using the hi-fi in the living room, and the so-called music blasted through the house all afternoon. The situation blew up one day.

"Turn that noise down!" Ah Dang shouted.

Ah Wei emerged from his bedroom next to the living room. Ah Dang noticed the sullen look, but the boy did turn the volume down, if only by a fraction, and retreated to his dark den.

Ah Dang relaxing while reading a Chinese newspaper, *circa* 1960s.

"I said turn it *down*! I can't even hear myself think. How can I read my newspaper?"

No response. Was the boy deliberately ignoring him? Furiously, Ah Dang lifted the needle arm, whipped off the record, and snapped it in two. Now it would be quiet. Ah Wei ran out at the sound of the breaking record, glared at him, and stomped out of the house, slamming the door. *He was reacting like a disrespectful Canadian boy!* Ah Dang fumed. Now it really *was* quiet. Ah Thloo had stayed in the kitchen throughout the incident, but his daughter had been watching from the couch, gazing at him with sadness.

It felt as though all his encounters with his son ended this way, in unresolved anger and silent recrimination from his wife and daughter. If he didn't do something soon, Ah Wei would be irretrievably lost in his foreign ways. Maybe it was time for the children to go to China to be reeducated. It was certainly time for his son to meet the girl with whom he had been corresponding over the past year—at least he had been obedient on that account. Also, Ah Thloo could see how their eldest child was faring and Ah May could meet her sister and Ah Ngange. Ah Thloo agreed it was for the best.

Ah Dang had to stay in Montreal to work. He would miss his little girl; she was his constant source of affection. Perhaps Ah Thloo would see his sacrifice and stop blaming him for their elder daughter's refusal to come to Canada. He bought three one-way tickets. He would let his wife assess the children's educational progress and determine how long they should stay.

o   o   o

AH THLOO, AH WEI, AND AH MAY: CHINA, 1966–1967

Who could have anticipated the Great Proletarian Cultural Revolution, which began in 1966? To launch the campaign, Chairman Mao Zedong swam across the feared Yangtze River. This feat, additional evidence of his superhuman abilities, cemented his cult status.

Student activists, aged nine to eighteen, acted as Mao's agents of social change. An estimated thirteen million urban youth volunteered as Red Guards, and from August to November 1966, they were transported free on trains and housed in Beijing, to attend eight rallies in Tiananmen Square.

Their fervour, stirred up by Mao's simplistic slogans—"Learn Revolution by Making Revolution" and "Seizure of Power"—was unleashed on his political opponents and "suspicious" citizens. Their common bible was a little red book, *Quotations of Chairman Mao*, and their common cause was to attack the "Four Olds—old ideas, old culture, old customs, old habits." The students were given little direction, leaving much room for misinformation, misinterpretation, and mistakes.

The Red Guards, identified by their armbands, roamed through the streets with impunity, like the bandits and thugs of old. Schools were closed, books were burned, and cultural institutions were ransacked. An unaccounted fortune was lost from the wanton destruction of cultural artifacts.

Traditional scholars, professionals, and others were publicly humiliated, tortured, and beaten in "struggle meetings," where victims were forced to "confess" in front of jeering crowds. For a people who value *hoo mien*, to have face, these public meetings were sometimes harder to bear than their physical pain.

Thousands were torn from their families and banished to distant and remote parts of the country to "reeducate" themselves through hard physical labour. Others were imprisoned or killed, or just vanished. Few families were spared, not even Ah Dang's.

When Mao finally admitted that the Red Guards were out of control, he sent the People's Liberation Army to round up the students for exile into the countryside. The Cultural Revolution was declared ended in April 1969. However, the overzealous army, and the notorious political manipulators known as the Gang of Four, continued the witch hunts, and committed additional atrocities over the next seven years.

By the end of "The Ten Lost Years," more than one million people had been victimized, of whom more than four hundred thousand died, many by suicide. A swath of mentally and physically broken people was left in the wake of the systematic cruelty inflicted throughout this period.

Ah Thloo, Ah Wei, and Ah May were unwittingly there to witness its beginning.

○   ○   ○

The first stop on the way to China was Hong Kong, where Ah Thloo's god-daughter, Ah Ngan Jean, met them at the airport. The women had a happy, if tearful reunion. Ah Wei and Ah May greeted Ah Ngan Jean enthusiastically; their mother had read her cheery, annual letters to them, but they recognized her from her photographs. In person, she looked like a movie star, with full lips, big eyes, coiffed hair, and a slim figure. Ah May also knew her as the sender of made-in-Hong Kong Disney paraphernalia as gifts; she already loved Ah Ngan Jean.

The next few weeks passed in a whirlwind of meeting family, sightseeing, eating, and shopping. Day and night they were bombarded by life in the island city. Even behind the door of their hotel room, every sense in their bodies continued to experience the residuals left by the flashing neon, blasting horns, diesel fumes, loud voices, glittering gold, pushy vendors, shiny jade, wet streets, smooth silks, medicinal herbs, tall buildings, armed guards, rich houses, poor shacks, rotting vegetables, fresh meat, live foods, impressive vistas, extreme crowding, lush gardens, and the most delicate and delicious dim sum they had ever eaten.

The train trip from Hong Kong to Guangzhou, China, was memorable for the anxiety-ridden delay at customs. The Wongs' Canadian passports were confiscated and the polite, armed officials disappeared with them while the family was made to wait at the station. Communication was difficult, as Ah Thloo did not speak Mandarin and the officials did not understand her dialect.

Since the revolution, the borders between China and the world had been tightly barricaded and closely monitored. Canada did not officially recognize the People's Republic of China or establish diplomatic relations with its government until 1970. Few tourists visited—in fact, the Wongs were among the first. If anything had happened to them, no diplomatic assistance would have been available; they were on their own.

Perhaps it *was* dangerous, and hindsight showed how precarious the political situation in China was in 1966. However, Ah May's parents, especially her mother, had faith—faith in God to keep them safe and faith in the government of the People's Republic to treat former peasants like her with respect.

Moments before the train was scheduled to leave, the documents were returned to Ah Thloo, and she and her children were finally allowed to board. They never knew the reasons for the delay. It might have been the normal process and it might have been a customs issue; they carried a lot of extra goods. In addition to their luggage from Canada, in Hong Kong they had bought bicycles, a sewing machine, blankets, electric fans, bolts of fabric, bags of dried foodstuffs, and myriad other useful household items for the extended family in China. No Chinese person ever made a social call empty-handed. Seasonal fruits were acceptable gifts, but Ah Thloo knew from Ah Lai's letters that many manufactured household items were difficult to obtain. The Wongs were ready to see anyone and provide a practical item for his or her enjoyment.

When they arrived in Guangzhou at last, Ah Thloo's youngest brother, Ah Choo, met the family at the station. Her head only reached up to his neck. His features were just like hers but elongated.

Ah Thloo, her brother Ah Choo, and Ah May eating dim sum in Guangzhou, 1966.
ROBERT WONG, CHINA

Ah Choo greeted everyone warmly, hugging his sister and patting his nephew on the back and his niece on the head. Ah Thloo also appeared happy to see her brother. Ah May did not expect anything different, not knowing, at the time, the history of his abandonment of her mother and sister during the war with Japan. He took them out to meals. After eating, he and Ah Thloo alternated paying, after the obligatory verbal and physical tug-of-war for the bill.

Ah Choo lived alone in the city, where he worked in construction, following in the footsteps of his father, Ah Poy Lim. By the time Ah Choo was ready to enter university, the economic situation in China had deteriorated to such an extent that his father could no longer afford to pay the fees. Instead, Ah Poy Lim took his youngest son with him wherever there were construction jobs, teaching the boy about building—the use of materials and tools, and the art of creating, and reading architectural plans—and passing on his knowledge and skills. Now Ah Choo was a construction foreman.

Ah Wei in Guangzhou, sporting his Mao hat, 1966.
MAY Q. WONG, CHINA

Ah Choo's wife and family lived in his parents' house in the village. While Ah Thloo and her family were in Guangzhou, he spent as much time with them as his work allowed. He missed his own children, who were about Ah May's age, so he took his nephew and niece under his wing.

Ah Thloo also took the children to meet her eldest sister, Ah Ngay Day, who lived with her son's widow and the grandchildren, in a fourth-floor apartment with no elevator. Ah May noticed that this aunt was also taller than her mother, but they had the same smile that lit up their eyes. Catching up on family news and exchanging photos, Ah Ngay Day gushed with delight at seeing the most recent photo of her new grandson in Montreal, the child of her youngest daughter, Ah Yee.

The three Wongs stayed at the official Overseas Chinese Hotel, close to the harbour. As they awaited the arrival of Ah Lai and her family in the hotel room, Ah Wei and Ah May watched their mother, who could not sit still. She rearranged the snacks, fidgeted with the embroidered antimacassars on the chairs, and jumped up at the slightest noise in the hall. They had never seen her act this way; they sat quietly, not knowing what to expect. When she opened the door to a tentative knock, the simultaneous screams of "Ah Maaah!" and "Ah Nuuui!" could be heard through the whole building. The youngsters did not understand the words that followed—both women were blubbering with hysterical happiness.

Ah Wei looked at Ah May with raised eyebrows. "What a sissy," he said, referring to his elder sister's sobbing. The nickname stuck. "Sissy" was the term they used whenever they referred (not unkindly) to their elder sister. When addressing her out loud, of course, they called her Ah Day.

Ah Lai's reaction to Ah Wei was the same—he was enveloped in a close hug, after an exuberant shout of "Ah Hai," Younger Brother. The last time she had seen him she could still piggyback him; now he was the taller than she was. Thinking about the last time they were in Guangzhou together, she started to cry again, but by the time she got to Ah May, she had had a chance to collect herself.

"Ah Day," Ah May said dutifully.

With a smile that rivalled the neon lights of Hong Kong, Ah Lai exclaimed, "Ah Moy!" and welcomed her little sister to the family and to China.

As the Canadian family was introduced to Ah Lai's family, Ah May developed an immediate crush on her sister's movie-star-handsome husband, Ah Haw One, and everyone fell under the spell of their adorable daughter, Ah Bing Fuy. Ah May even let the three-year-old play with her prized doll from Canada. Ah Lai, now a medical doctor, and her university professor husband had taken a special leave to meet and escort the Wongs back to their home near Wuhan. But first, they planned to stay a few days in Guangzhou and then travel with their Canadian relatives to the family hamlet. Citizens were not allowed to stay in the Overseas Chinese Hotel, so Ah Choo offered Ah Lai and her family his small apartment while he moved in with a friend.

o   o   o

Guangzhou has many public gardens, full of elegant old trees and tall pagodas. The Wongs' first glimpse of the Cultural Revolution occurred in one of the most beautiful of these gardens. As they strolled by a particularly ornate pagoda, surrounded by a group of Red Guards, they looked up several storeys. More students had crowded into the building and a number leaned out the windows, holding large, beautiful porcelain vases in their hands. In response to challenging shouts from below, the hands opened wide, dropping the antiques onto the gravel. A roar of triumph followed each vase as it shattered, spraying shards of fine pottery in a thousand directions.

The family was not close enough to be injured by the sharp ceramic missiles, but from where they stood, momentarily riveted by the vandalism, they felt the tension and smelled the adrenalin-induced sweat of the mob. Even at the age of ten, Ah May was shocked at the destruction of the pieces of artwork, more outraged than afraid. The adults, however, understood the threat and hurried back to the hotel, where they conferred on what to do to secure everyone's safety.

The next day, at Ah Choo's house, Ah Thloo told Ah May their decision. Her Barbie doll and all her clothes would have to be destroyed. The toy's pale, full-figured female shape was just too dangerous to keep; it would be seen as an example of depraved foreign capitalist culture and anyone associated with such an item was in grave peril.

"NO—not by fire! I'll keep it hidden. I'll never take it out again," Ah May protested and cried. Her pleading fell on ears hardened by the wax of determination; safety was her mother's priority.

It was like watching a horror movie. Ah May had not wanted to witness the destruction of her beloved companion, but the process fascinated her.

"Wow! Did you see the hair just flare up and disappear? Like *woof*—and that was it!" said Ah Wei.

"Shhh, be quiet!" Ah Thloo looked sternly at him through the door. "Can't you do this any faster?"

Ah Wei tossed items of colourful clothing into the flames, each piece flashing briefly before turning into grey ash. The youngsters gazed, mesmerized, as the rounded breasts became tipped with smoky nipples and the torso of the doll blackened, warped, and melted into ooze.

Luckily, no one came by to use the kitchen. Their mother's prayers had been heard.

o   o   o

The trip back to the hamlet where Ah Ngange lived was long, hot, smelly, and dusty. From Guangzhou, the family had transferred from a crowded bus to an overnight boat, where everyone slept on its hard deck, trying not to choke on the black diesel smoke spewing from its smokestack. At the ferry dock, some young men from the hamlet came to meet the group and carry back the heavy loads. Ah Wei thought he recognized some of them as his former childhood playmates, but didn't say anything.

They all walked the final leg of the journey, hauling the bags with clothes and gifts along the precarious, narrow, raised dirt paths bordering the wet rice paddies. They were reversing the trip Ah Wei, his mother, and his grandmother had made thirteen years earlier. Ah May kept asking, "How much farther?" Ah Wei kept searching the distance, looking for Ah Ngange.

As they neared their destination, it was Ah Thloo who pointed to a small, stooped figure in the distance. The person, with a child riding piggyback, seemed to be waiting for them. The child's feet almost touched the ground. Ah Wei recognized her at once, although she was not the same person in his memory. *She is so small—how could someone shrink so much in such a short time?*

"There is Ah Ngange," his mother said. "At her advanced age and still carrying children!"

Ah Ngange acknowledged Ah Thloo by saying, "You've returned, have

Left to right: Ah One, Ah May, Ah Lai, and Ah Ngange (seated), Ah Thloo
holding granddaughter Ah Fuy, and Ah Wei, in Longe Gonge Lay, 1966.
UNKNOWN PHOTOGRAPHER, CHINA

you?" and pointed to Ah May. "Is this *aie may nui*?" Ah Ngange had used a
play on her name; "aie may" was the phrase meaning "last."

"Ah Ngange," Ah May said at her mother's gentle nudge.

Ah Ngange only nodded solemnly at her greeting but smiled warmly at
their elder sister, Ah Lai, and her family, obviously delighted to see them
again. Ah Fuy hid behind her father's pant legs. While Ah Wei put his packages down, his elder sister rushed forward to greet Ah Ngange. He and Ah
May exchanged an eye roll and a conspiratorial smile as their sister started
to cry again.

Turning her attention to Ah Wei at last, Ah Ngange exclaimed, "My
Gowdoy, look how you have grown!"

Ah Wei swept up his grandmother in a hug so powerful that he lifted
her into the air, even with the child strapped onto her back. Ah Ngange
laughed out loud, but when her feet touched the ground again, she became
serious, rearranged the child in the sling, turned around, and led the way
back to the house.

At the hamlet, a swarm of smiling, wrinkled, gap-toothed, and sun-browned faces emerged from the houses to greet the family. News of the Canadians' arrival had travelled via the bamboo telegraph; people had even come from the surrounding villages. The neighbours knew the family had not come empty-handed—there would be gift-giving and feasting over the next few days. Some of the villagers had already brought welcoming gifts of dim sum dumplings, oranges, and sugar cane. The women helped prepare food while the men hauled water from the well for cooking and cleaning and arranged tables and chairs. The children brought kindling for the stove.

Ah Wei left the house, eager to see everything and to test his childhood memories against the reality. Ah May followed him as he gave her a tour of the building and its surroundings and pointed out his favourite spots. At the back of the house was an old tree, its two main branches dividing to create a comfortable seat for a child. Ah Wei remembered spending count-less hours in the leafy perch, but looking at it now, he thought the tree might have been trimmed down over the years. He took a picture of Ah May in his old lookout. Nearby was the bamboo garden, where their elder sister had shredded the flesh on her hands, collecting and shaving bamboo into strips.

The house was large, much bigger than their Montreal home, yet the living room was used only after dark, when the mosquitoes started biting. During the day, all the feasting took place outside because so many people had come.

Upstairs, Ah Wei showed Ah May the wooden bed in their parents' room, where she would sleep with their mother. His sister made a face, showing her disgust, when he told her this was the bed on which he had been born. Most of the beds in the house consisted of wooden planks laid over crossbars on a wooden frame. A light, quilted blanket served as the only mattress. Their parents' bed was made of woven bamboo strips, set in a wooden frame. It was thought to be superior for comfort and coolness, but when the siblings tested it, they felt the lumps created by the woven bamboo, inadequately padded by the quilts. It was not like their beds at home in Montreal. The next morning, even their mother had found it dif-ficult to get a restful sleep and was out of bed before the cocks crowed. She gave Ah May the excuse of having too much work to do and being excited at seeing her old friends and neighbours.

Poking through the rooms, Ah Wei and Ah May found some striped Hudson's Bay blankets their father had brought from Canada, stored in a mothball-filled, metal-sided shipping trunk. Hanging on a wall peg was the long chain of tien, copper coins, which had accompanied their mother on her bridal journey to this hamlet. The coins, with square holes cut out of the middle, were still tied together with faded, fraying red string. Ah Wei cut off some of the discs as keepsakes.

Beside the stairwell sat the large, colourful family shrine. At the opposite end of the landing were doors that led to the safe room on the deck from which their mother had told them she had shot at bandits. They found a cat there, curled up and sleeping peacefully in the sunshine.

The next few days were filled with social gatherings and new faces. Every meal was a feast; the people all talked at the same time, exclaiming their surprise at Ah Wei's height, asking about life in Ga-Na-Aie. It was hard for him to understand them, and he couldn't remember the appropriate words to answer their questions. He could see the younger village kids snickering behind their hands at his lack of Chinese and he was grateful that his younger sister and their precocious niece were able to attract some of the attention away from him.

Ah Wei was especially anxious about one event. He was to finally meet Huo Li Sheung, the girl his parents were hoping he would marry. They had been corresponding for the past year, had exchanged photographs, and, through his mother's letters, had got to know each other a little. The whole family accompanied him to her village, for she was related to his brother-in-law, Ah Haw One. She was already family. After everyone was introduced, Ah Wei and Ah Sheung were left to spend time alone for a few hours.

Ah Sheung was prettier in person than in her pictures. She did not seem to mind his hesitant Chinese and waited patiently while he spoke. She had a good sense of humour that even he could understand and the afternoon flashed by. He definitely liked her and thought she liked him too. They agreed to keep corresponding. He vowed to learn more Chinese—it had been awkward and embarrassing to have his mother as a go-between. For Ah Wei, the visit ended too soon.

Ah May, though, could not wait to get back to the city, where there were toilets and hot running water. She had cried each time she had to use the large, outdoor ceramic pot that served as a communal latrine, afraid of touching it and even more afraid of falling in. She had been plagued by the mosquitoes and her body was covered in itchy, red welts. She was glad she had not been born in the hamlet, and now, more than ever, missed her home in Montreal.

Ah Lai and her husband had to go back to Wuhan to work, and everyone took leave of Ah Ngange, with prolonged and mournful farewells; the only dry-eyed person was the old lady herself. Before heading north, the six family members travelled back to Guangzhou, to pick up the items from Hong Kong that were stored at Ah Choo's apartment.

Three months later, Ah Ngange packed all her worldly possessions into a single suitcase, and with her cat safely enclosed in a metal cage, locked the house for the last time. The two of them made the long journey to Wuhan. Ah Wei rode his bicycle through the pouring rain to the train station to meet Ah Ngange and tied her suitcase and cat cage on to his handlebars. Sitting on a carrier mounted above his back wheel, she clung on to him tightly with both arms. When they finally arrived at Ah Lai's apartment an hour later, she was soaked and frozen stiff. It was Ah Wei's turn to pick up his grandmother, and, cradling her tiny, shivering body up the stairs and over the threshold, he welcomed her to her new home.

The cat, her mouser, was intended as a gift for the family, to be consumed in a prized and nourishing broth.

o o o

The Wongs moved into Ah Lai's small apartment in Donghu, East Lake, near Wuhan. This area in northeast China was famous for its silk, Shaoxing rice wine, and cotton. It was scorching hot in the summer and freezing in the winter, but its homes had neither air conditioning nor central heating.

Donghu is a man-made lake, surrounded by elegant weeping willows and landscaped into a tranquil garden. The largest lake within a Chinese city, it covers eighty-seven square kilometres and is dotted with pagodas along scenic bays. The part of the park Ah May was most familiar with had mature bamboo forests, stone sculpture gardens, and displays of enormous clay pots filled with exotic goldfish sprouting elaborate fins, tails, and eyes. It was a safe playground, where she rode her brother's bicycle and where she and Ah Fuy, her niece, climbed the large stone elephants standing throughout the park.

Watching Ah Fuy ride the elephant at Donghu. Ah Lai is pregnant.

H.B. GUAN, CHINA

Although Ah May did not know it then, also on the property was Chairman Mao's villa, where he spent time during his latter years. However, the main complex within the grounds was a secure, military, convalescent hospital and home for the aged. Survivors of the Long March, considered national heroes, were cared for there. This was the hospital where Ah Lai worked as an internist.

Ah Lai's wages included housing and food coupons. Her mother and her two siblings shared her two-bedroom apartment with her daughter, her mother-in-law, and Ah Ngange. Ah Haw One boarded at the university and came home on the weekends. In the main bedroom, Ah May shared one bed with their mother while Ah Lai and Ah Fuy shared another. The mother-in-law and Ah Ngange slept on separate cots in the living room. Until Ah Wei enrolled at the boarding school, he had the smaller bedroom to himself. Afterwards, Ah Ngange was moved in there. Ah Thloo paid an extra stipend for rent and food coupons.

The two-storey brick building housed members of the hospital's medical staff and their families. Every household had children, a number of whom were Ah May's age. Just as she had growing up in Montreal, she learned to speak the common language by playing with the neighbours' children. Here, it was Mandarin Chinese; she even picked up the local Wuhan accent. In a ground-floor apartment lived an elderly woman with bound feet. The mother of one of the nurses, she was a cheerful soul, hobbling gamely after her lively, two-year-old grandson. Ah May remembered the stories her mother told about her own grandmother, and was fascinated by how well the woman could get around.

Each apartment had a small kitchen with a wood-fired cooking hearth, a sink, and a cold-water tap. In the summer heat, all the doors and windows were left open to catch any possible breeze. Unfortunately, the fans bought in Hong Kong only moved the hot, dry air around in gusts, and did nothing to cool the apartment or its inhabitants. Heat in winter came from a coal-burning stove in the living room. Its efficiency was compromised because a door had to be kept open to prevent suffocation from carbon monoxide fumes; everyone still had to bundle up. On the beds, the cotton quilts were piled three and four layers high; they were so heavy it was hard to roll over. Ah May was glad to have her mother to snuggle up to during the winter.

The children wore cotton-stuffed clothes that made them look like mini-Bonhommes de Neige, the giant snowman mascot of Quebec's Winter Carnival and Montreal's Christmas parade. Ah Fuy wore Ah May's old woollen coat over her quilted jacket, which made the little girl's bulky arms stick out at ninety degrees from her body.

The communal wash areas and multi-seat outhouse were in separate wooden buildings, a short distance behind the apartment. The washing room had several sinks along the wall, with only a cold-water tap, but the single shower that sprouted multiple heads, at the centre of the room, was connected to a water heater. Women and men were each allotted a separate evening during the week to enjoy hot showers.

The daily routine was the same for everyone. Each morning at six, the loudspeakers blasted out "The East Is Red," a rousing revolutionary song. The patriotic music would continue until it was interrupted by news bulletins and other propaganda. Ah Lai made the twenty-minute return trek to the hospital commissary to buy breakfast foods of jook, rice soup, or *man how*, freshly steamed bread rolls, which were eaten with a delicious spread of ground sesame paste.

If it were a "market" day, that is, when the only store in the area had supplies of fresh meat or vegetables, someone from the family had to go to the store before the wake-up call, to wait in line with the food coupons. Ah Thloo took on this chore, as she had extra coupons. She had no trouble arguing with the proprietor about her right to buy extra food. It was a very bourgeois attitude, but she ignored the hostile stares, pointing fingers, and nasty words flung her way. Besides, she was deaf to the Mandarin Chinese dialect they spoke.

Ah May and her brother were finally enrolled—she in the local elementary school, he in a boarding school a few hours' bike ride away. They attended classes for only a month, however; as the Cultural Revolution progressed, their schools were closed. Institutions of learning were considered to be repositories of "old thinking." For Ah May, this attitude was shocking, as her parents had always instilled in her a reverence for learning, but Ah Wei, now eighteen, had heard his Canadian friends talk about the burgeoning anti-establishment movement in Montreal, so he was not totally surprised to hear something similar happening in China.

Students and teachers were "sent down" to the countryside to be "reeducated" by peasants. When Ah May told Ah Thloo her class of students was going away, her mother did not seem worried, so the girl felt safe and thought of it as a long camp-out, although no one knew the schedule, location, or plan of action beforehand.

The students walked for a day, in orderly lineups, singing patriotic songs, to reach the cotton fields where they were to work. The cotton bushes were about three feet high, planted in straight rows across a never-ending field. Picking cotton was backbreaking work. Cotton bols sprouted in clusters all over the bush; Ah May had to bend close to the ground and reach through the branches, to pick the bushes clean. The soft white balls, many infested with small, pink worms, were tucked within dried, dark brown husks that curled open like tiger lilies. The hard, sharp points of the shells pricked fingers and scratched any exposed skin. A full basket, the size of a utility pail, was surprisingly heavy. The daily physical exertion kept Ah May from worrying about her surroundings.

After a long day's work, with short breaks for tea and meals, there were evening meetings, with lectures based on *Quotations of Chairman Mao*. In his book, Mao explained his theory of emancipation for the peasants of China.

Ah May was excused from the evening lectures; with her limited Mandarin, her teachers knew she would not have understood a thing. It was still early days in the Cultural Revolution, and the zealots had not all emerged.

The students were housed in a shed that had been converted from a byre; the stalls were filled with fresh straw, on which thin blankets were spread. A huge sow and her litter shared the space with the children, separated from them only by a thin, shaky, wooden wall, which shuddered whenever the pig rolled over. If Ah May had not been so hot, dirty, lonely, and muscle-crampingly tired, she would have worried all night about being squashed to death by that pig. She lost track of time, but after about a week, the group trekked back home. Ah May did not feel any better "educated" than when she had first arrived, but she did not share that thought with her classmates.

Ah Wei's school had also gone on a work outing for an extended period. Curiously, Ah Thloo, who had worried when Ah May attended a birthday party at a schoolmate's house a block down the street in Montreal, never worried about the whereabouts of either of her younger children while they were in China. She retained her memories of being rescued from oppression by the Communists, led by Mao. Having idealized and romanticized the recent past, she dismissed the incidents with the Red Guards in Guangzhou as being unusual. She might have been trying to protect Ah Wei and Ah May, to shield them from fear, but even talking about it decades later, she insisted she had never fretted about their safety.

When the students returned to Donghu, it was clear that none of the schools would be reopened, so Ah Thloo took Ah Wei and Ah May on another kind of educational tour—it was time to see their nation's capital. They joined a group of Chinese tourists, all returned from foreign lands. The tour was led by a small, kindly, neatly dressed man who spoke a number of Chinese dialects and foreign languages, including English. His name, coincidentally, was Mr. Wong.

In Beijing, the group took in the usual sights—the Great Wall, Tiananmen Square, the Forbidden City, the Great Hall of the People, the Ming Tombs, and a performance of the Beijing Opera. They stayed at the Overseas Chinese Hotel and shopped at the exclusive International Service Department Store for souvenirs; neither of these places allowed comrade-citizens to stay or shop.

In 1966, the rooms and many of the artifacts in the Forbidden City were much more accessible than they are today, and there were no foreign-owned, profit-making concessions. At the opera, instead of an imperial play featuring emperors such as Ah Thloo used to watch on film in Montreal, there was a performance of *The White Haired Girl*. It was a revolutionary opera about a peasant girl whose hair turns white after she is raped and forced to watch the brutal killing of her family by an evil landlord. She becomes his slave, but is set free by gentle, revolutionary soldiers and ends up a war heroine.

In addition to the usual tourist stops, the group was also taken to places that highlighted China's growing industrial sectors. In a steel-making plant, the tourists wended their way along overhead catwalks, and felt the heat emanating from red-hot molten metal being poured into moulds, while they were lectured about production capacity and safety records. The pig-slaughtering factory was extolled as a model of efficiency and for Ah May became fodder for years of bloody nightmares.

During this time, the family was protected from the dangers that came later, as the Cultural Revolution progressed and anarchy reigned among the undisciplined students. Perhaps the officials recognized their country of origin as that of the revered Dr. Norman Bethune, a Canadian doctor who gave his life during the revolution. His likeness, and those of other heroes such as Lenin, was prominently displayed everywhere on giant posters, sculptures, and reliefs. Looking back, Ah May could only conjecture that the tourists in their group were treated royally and fêted as first-hand witnesses to the greatness that had again blossomed in China so that when they returned to their respective homelands, they could be unofficial ambassadors.

o   o   o

"*Aiya*! I never dreamed that one day I would be eating a banquet in the Great Hall of the People! There I was, a child of poor farmers, living in a foreign country, sitting with Premier Zhou Enlai!" said Ah Thloo.

Ah Thloo's eyes never failed to light up, nor did her sense of awe and wonder ever diminish when she reminisced about this event. To her friends at church back in Montreal, she always recounted the experiences of her first trip back to China with excitement, but as she spoke about one particular night, her face beamed with delight that lasted long past the telling.

Crowds cheering for Mao Zedong at Tiananmen Gate on National Day, 1966.
ROBERT WONG, CHINA

The occasion was the anniversary of the creation of the People's Republic of China: October 1, a national holiday. Earlier that day, Ah Thloo, Ah Wei, and Ah May had been in the crush of the hundreds of thousands of Red Guards and comrades lining Tiananmen Square to watch the grand parade. It was claustrophobic, noisy, and frightening, but also exhilarating.

They had witnessed the might of the Communist regime, as a miles-long wall of armoured cars, tanks, and other machinery of war drove slowly through the huge square, followed by troops marching with precision. The music from the speakers ricocheted off the large, squat buildings surrounding the square, adding to the overall commotion.

The mounting pride and excitement of the masses of people around the family was infectious. It was hard not to be caught up in the chanting and waving as the parade progressed down the wide avenue. Everyone was waiting for a glimpse of Chairman Mao, whose appearances were tightly controlled and orchestrated. Above the crowd was a sea of waving hands, holding dog-eared copies of *Quotations of Chairman Mao*, the holy book, from which phrases and even whole chapters could be recited like incantations.

Chandelier in Banquet Hall of Beijing's Great Hall of the People, 1966.
ROBERT WONG, CHINA

Ah Thloo and the youngsters joined the chanting, "May Chairman Mao live ten thousand years, ten thousand, ten thousand years!" They were urging him to come onto the balcony of Tiananmen Gate to grace them with an appearance. Suddenly, there he was, and although the Wongs were far away, they knew who it was, because the crowd roared, swayed, and jumped in overwhelming passion. Wave after wave of deafening, joyful, worshipful human voices rushed over them, around them, and through them.

When the family returned to the hotel later that afternoon, Ah Wei and Ah May were physically and mentally exhausted. Their bodies had been squeezed and twisted by the frenzied throngs, their ears rang, and their backs, legs, and feet hurt from standing all day. They needed hot baths and naps.

But Ah Thloo did not show any signs of fatigue. She was as excited as if she were lit from inside. She had seen the prosperity the Communists had created, the adoration of the chairman by the people, and the show of military force that declared China to be a great nation once again.

She told her children, "*Nah*, see! See how great Chairman Mao is! He liberated the Chinese from foreign domination. We can hold our heads high no matter where we are in the world. We no longer have to be ashamed of being Chinese. Our family owes him so much. Your sister could not have become a doctor. Your grandmother can now look forward to a restful old age, without having to scramble for food and kindling every day."

Ah Thloo had apparently forgotten the long lineups in Donghu for tightly rationed food and commodities the family in Canada had considered ordinary. Many decades later, after she had read about the atrocities of the Cultural Revolution and learned of the dangers faced by her older daughter and her family, she developed a more realistic opinion of Mao. But at the time, she was extremely proud to be Chinese and to be in China with her children.

So it was incredible that Mr. Wong had invitations for all the adults in the tour group to celebrate the evening's festivities at the Great Hall of the People. The building had impressive dimensions, with a frontage that extended more than three hundred and thirty-five metres, or two city blocks. Inside, the floor space measured more than five hundred and sixty thousand square metres. Its meeting hall had more than ten thousand seats, and the banquet room, where Ah Thloo and Ah Wei ate, could accommodate five thousand people.

Ah May was too young, so she had to stay behind, where she reluctantly joined the few other youngsters in the tour group for a special dinner prepared by the hotel's restaurant. When Ah Thloo came back much later that evening, she recounted every detail of the banquet to her daughter. "*Ooy*! We were in the very same room with Premier Zhou Enlai! Of course, we didn't sit together, but we were served the same food—everything was the same as the premier's. He was so handsome. Even though we sat far away, I could tell he looked just like his pictures in the *China News Magazine*."

Ah Thloo stopped and smiled at this point, an enigmatic look that Ah May did not understand. Shaking her head she added, "Did you see the van that came to the hotel to pick us up? It dropped us right at the front door, behind the guards. We felt like movie stars on TV!"

The banquet hall was filled with round tables, each covered with a starched white tablecloth and set for twelve people. Everything glittered, lit by the large ceiling chandeliers—red stars surrounded by golden sunflower petals. Ah Thloo had listened politely to the myriad speeches but could not recall what was said; after each speaker, she did remember the sound made by thousands of clapping hands and described it to Ah May as *pock, pock, pock, pock*—like a hailstorm on a hot summer day.

The food was never ending. As soon as the guests had started tasting one course, another plate was delivered to the table. Ah Thloo's favourite dish was the Peking duck, which she described with relish. "At first, we were presented with the delicate pieces of golden brown, crispy skin. We ate it with tender green scallions, all folded in small thin pancakes spread with sweet hoisin sauce. Then came the moist pieces of meat, wrapped in fresh lettuce leaves, while the inner organs were sautéed in a spicy sauce and presented separately. The bones were used to prepare a broth; nothing I have ever tasted can compare to the flavour of that marvellous soup!

"I got a special feeling from the fireworks. We Chinese invented fireworks, but when I was young, only the empress, landlords, and foreigners could use them. Chairman Mao made it possible for everyone to enjoy them. Even though our table was all from overseas, we were treated like guests of the highest honour!"

When Ah Thloo and the children returned to Wuhan, the schools were still closed and would continue to be for several years. For a while, within the Donghu community, they were cocooned from the outside world. News was tightly controlled, but people were getting nervous.

In Montreal, news of the Red Guard rallies, the rampages, and the destruction was leaking out. The reports indicated that all foreigners, or people with relatives in foreign countries, were being mistreated. The minister and others at the church, who had been against the family going to China in the first place, were strongly pressuring Ah Dang to get them out of the country.

By then, Ah Lai was pregnant again and would have enjoyed having her mother and her siblings meet the new baby, but she and her husband were resigned to having them return to Canada. Her mother's behaviour at the market would have targeted her for political scrutiny and perhaps reeducation. It was beginning to be dangerous.

Ah Thloo and the youngsters left Ah Lai, her growing family, and Ah Ngange in January 1967, less than a year after they had arrived. The tension at the border going out was even worse than when they went in. The Red Guards were everywhere and they had tasted the power of zealotry. The family tried to look nonchalant and when questioned told the guards as little as possible about their relatives in China.

They stayed in Hong Kong for another few weeks, where they met Ah Ngan Jean's new baby girl, Susan. On the day they left for Canada, Ah Ngan Jean, other family members, and, surprisingly, their China tour guide, Mr. Wong, were at the airport to see them off.

All beings and things are in a dynamic state of change and transformation; nothing in the universe is absolutely static or completed; all is in unceasing motion because polarization, the source of being, is without beginning and without end.

—Hua-Ching Ni, *Tao: The Subtle Universal Law and the Integral Way of Life*

THIRTEEN ·
Successes and Setbacks

◯

AH DANG: MONTREAL, 1970

When most men might have been retired at sixty-eight, Ah Dang was still building on his success as a restaurateur. However, he had one more accomplishment to add to his businessman's persona—he needed a car. As soon as he completed his driving lessons and got his licence, he bought a brand-new sedan. The car, a rich royal blue, was like a land yacht—long and wide. With two bench seats, it could accommodate six adults comfortably. The trunk, when opened, was like the maw of a hungry dragon at New Year's.

Sitting in the driver's seat, he could see just above the dash; anyone looking into the car from behind saw the crown of a grey fedora and not much else of the driver's head. He could not quite see the back end of the car, neither in his rear-view mirror nor by turning his head, but he was not worried—hadn't he learned to use his side mirrors at the driver-training school?

o   o   o

Ah Dang is a proud restaurateur, 1950s.
UNKNOWN PHOTOGRAPHER, MONTREAL

AH THLOO: MONTREAL, 1967–1978

Ah Thloo, Ah Wei, and Ah May returned to Montreal in February 1967. After the eight-month trip to China, Ah Thloo was pragmatic enough to realize she would not be able to live there. Things had changed too much and the Cultural Revolution was making life for returned foreigners very dangerous; it could be worse if the Red Guards continued to have their way.

Ah Thloo decided her destiny lay in Canada—her son and younger daughter needed her more than Ah Lai. She had also confirmed with her own eyes that her elder daughter's *tange fong*, living conditions, in China were relatively safe, and thereafter, she ceased to cry with fear and guilt. However, Ah Thloo was still feeling uneasy about the difficult question of Ah Lai's identity papers.

"Paper sons" and "paper daughters" were children who emigrated bearing someone else's identity. Returning sojourners and their children who were born overseas might sell their identification papers when they returned to China, if the original holders had decided to stay in China or had died.

In 1959, one of Ah Dang's friends had come to him for help. The man wanted to bring his daughter to Canada, but because he was not yet naturalized, he could not sponsor her. He knew Ah Dang had listed his daughter on his citizenship application. The Canadian age limit had been raised to twenty-five and Ah Lai, then twenty-four, was still eligible to immigrate. Ah Dang, knowing how much Ah Thloo still missed their daughter, actually discussed this issue with his wife. They agreed that because Ah Lai had refused to come just a few years earlier, it was unlikely she would change her mind about leaving her grandmother and fiancé so soon. Also, she was still in medical college.

The papers were going to expire without being used, so Ah Dang reasoned it was a shame to deny his friend a family reunion. His own dream of seeing his whole family together in Canada was now out of reach, but he had tasted the loneliness of forced separation and had the means to prevent the same thing from happening to his friend. True, it was illegal, and if he were caught, he and his family could be in jeopardy. Reluctantly, Ah Dang gave the man the right to use Ah Lai's identification for his daughter.

Ah Thloo would have told their daughter, if she had asked, but she did not feel it necessary otherwise, as it might make her feel unwanted or unloved. Fortunately, while Ah Thloo was in China, the issue of Ah Lai's family going to Canada was never brought up. It was considered unpatriotic in the extreme to even think about leaving the country; applying for an exit visa would have targeted the family for unwanted suspicion and scrutiny. Ah Thloo felt she had dodged a bullet.

Back in Montreal, the Chinese Presbyterian Church continued to provide social, cultural, and spiritual sustenance for Ah Thloo and her family. With the exception of Ah Dang, who worked, the family still spent every week-end there. Ah Thloo threw herself into the work of the Women's Missionary Society (WMS). In addition to her responsibilities as the kitchen organizer for the church's annual tea, she sang in the women's choir, performed in Christmas concerts, and was an advocate on church policies. She spent hours on the telephone with the members of the WMS, discussing the merits of proposed new plans and developing strategies to get their positions accepted by the church's governing body. She built a reputation for getting things done; her opinions were sought after and respected.

Ah Thloo had come back to Canada when its economy was reaching a post-war peak; the mood was optimistic and confident. Prime Minister Lester B. Pearson introduced universal health care, the Canada Pension Plan, the Maple Leaf flag, and the world's first race-free immigration system. Between 1961 and 1971, Canada's Chinese population more than doubled.

To celebrate Canada's Centennial, Montreal was the site for the Universal and International Exhibition, known as Expo '67; its theme was "Man and His World." During one hundred and eighty-three days, from April to October, more than fifty million visitors, including queens, kings, presidents, and prime ministers, came to Montreal.

Ah Dang bought a season's passport for each family member, and during that summer the family spent every *offu day*, his day off work, together at Expo. Ah Thloo considered herself an experienced world traveller and was now excited to have the world come to her. On her return to Canada from China, she had at first been alarmed by the long-haired hippie counter-culture. Girls screaming on *The Ed Sullivan Show*, wearing scandalously short skirts and bright makeup, were especially shocking after she had lived among the strictly enforced uniformed austerity of China. However, she was so relieved at having escaped the Red Guards that she let Ah May attend the fair accompanied only by her friends. She could not help but reflect on the stark contrast between the way change was happening in China, with indiscriminate destruction, and the peaceful celebration of new technology at Expo.

Ah Thloo wanted to see everything and, not wishing to be hampered by her husband's interests, she visited Expo regularly with her church friend, Mrs. Leung. At eighty, Mrs. Leung was a capable, fun-loving widow. Having survived decades running a restaurant with her husband as the only Chinese couple in a small rural Quebec town, she spoke English and French. Both women were small and looked unassuming. Armed with her wide-brimmed, straw Chinese farmer's hat, a folding camp stool with a pouch that held her lunch, a thermos of tea, an umbrella, toilet paper, and her Expo passport, Ah Thloo worked her formidable strategy for quickly advancing in even the longest lineups. While Mrs. Leung did not have to pretend she was old, they both somehow convinced people in the middle of the line that they were too feeble to start waiting at the end. If anyone protested, and amazingly only a few did, they would sit on their stools and pretend they could not hear or understand. Shamelessly, they got into all the pavilions in record time.

○   ○   ○

AH DANG: MONTREAL, 1967–1978

Ah Dang was relieved that Ah Thloo and the children had returned to Canada safely, though the situation between husband and wife had not changed significantly. He told her he had missed them; their separation had reminded him too much of his lonely, enforced bachelor's life, and for a brief period, they did not argue. But he kept on working the night shift; it was easier on everyone.

Ah Dang's one constant, affectionate relationship was with Ah May. He always looked forward to seeing her, for she never hesitated to greet him with a loving hug at the beginning and end of his workdays. He also came to depend on her to translate official documents, and she even completed his annual income tax returns.

With Ah Thloo, he settled into a new pattern of communication, using their daughter as an intermediary. "Tell you mada . . ." was less stressful than initiating a direct conversation with his wife. If he said "white," she would say "black," but the messages from his wife seemed less demanding when the words were filtered through their daughter. In this they had common ground, as Ah Thloo felt exactly the same way.

It was easy for Ah May to become complicit, for it helped to calm the domestic atmosphere. She loved them both and wanted peace in the house, but it didn't always work. She watched as her mother muttered and stewed over a misunderstanding or disagreement, while her father, quick to anger, was just as quick to forget an episode, all within moments. Afterwards, he would smile conspiratorially, shake his head, and say, "You mada . . ," lean back in his recliner, and resume reading his newspaper. When Ah Thloo noticed his reaction, her anger would be stoked anew, and she would accuse him of dismissing her opinions. If Ah May tried to calm Ah Thloo, her mother fumed, "You always take your father's side!"

The relationship between Ah Dang and his son remained as delicate as a cobweb in winter. Ah Dang's dream was that none of his children would ever have to work in the restaurant business—the hours were too long and the work too hard. He wanted them to be educated so they could have professional jobs. He was proud of his elder daughter, who had chosen medicine as her career, but the career path for Ah Wei was neither clear-cut nor smooth.

Not long before the family went to China, Ah Wei had noted some developmental abnormalities and was diagnosed with Klinefelter's syndrome, a congenital defect that affected his physical and emotional development as well as his cognitive abilities. He found it hard to concentrate; academic learning was difficult and he failed to graduate from high school. Sensitive, artistic, and creative, he enjoyed working with his hands. Photography was a growing interest, and in this he had taken after his father. Ah Wei had recorded the trip to China on his palm-sized camera and had developed hundreds of miniature black-and-white photos. But neither art nor photography school were viable alternatives, in Ah Dang's opinion. Hadn't the boy's uncle studied art? It hadn't got him far—he never made a living as an artist.

Neither parent understood their son's difficulties and neither knew how to seek help. It was nobody's fault, but it was hard not to assign blame. Ah Thloo blamed her husband for not having been at home to provide guidance when their son was younger. Ah Dang blamed his wife for being overprotective. Ah Thloo resorted to prayer. Ah Dang gave his son a job at the restaurant, hoping that hard work would force him out of his "mood."

The red brick building constitutes the 1240-1246 block of Stanley Street, 2004.
MAY Q. WONG, MONTREAL

In November 1970, the directors of the China Garden Café Ltd. bought the 1240-1246 block on Stanley Street. It cost two hundred and sixty-five thousand dollars, with ninety-five thousand dollars down. The remainder was mortgaged at 7.75 per cent till 1987. The partners now owned their building as well as the successful restaurant. To help offset the mortgage, they collected rent from the apartments upstairs and from the other two businesses at street level.

Ah Dang now had money to spend on a toy, which he decided would be a car. As with all his major purchases, he selected the vehicle on his own. At home, he showed off the new vehicle to his family and their neighbours, strutting around it like a proud peacock displaying his feathers. He picked up Ah Thloo from the house and drove her downtown. It was his day off, but he couldn't wait to show the car to his colleagues at work. Sitting in the front for the first time with her husband in the driver's seat, Ah Thloo was petrified. She dared not say anything for fear of distracting him from his driving.

Everyone, even the cooks, came out to admire the car, inhaling deeply its new smell, caressing the shiny paint, and sitting behind the huge steering wheel. As they all swarmed around and through the automobile, Ah Thloo was served tea and almond cookies inside the restaurant. Gratified by their universal approval, Ah Dang collected his wife and prepared for a grand departure. His partners stood outside to watch and say goodbye. Waving, he stepped on the gas to pull out.

"*Eeee* . . . no, no, no!" was as much as Ah Thloo could get out before they heard a sharp *Caa* . . . *rack*! and both husband and wife were thrown back suddenly in their seats. A split-second later, they heard the tinkling of shattered glass showering down on the back of their pristine car.

For a sixty-eight-year-old, his reflexes were pretty good—he stepped on the brake as soon as he heard his wife call out. But he was not quite quick enough to stop the car from backing into the plate-glass window of his restaurant. Stunned and humiliated, his blood pressure soaring, Ah Dang was determined not to be cowed. After dealing with insurance adjusters for both the restaurant and the car, he drove home. Ah Thloo was even more terrified and clutched the door handle all the way to the house, as if preparing to jump out. He never drove again.

Ah Dang retired in 1978, at the age of seventy-six. The limited company was dissolved on November 8, 1986, and the assets sold, whereupon the rest of his original partners also retired.

o   o   o

AH LAI: WUHAN, 1967–1976

While the situation in 1966 had felt relatively safe for Ah Lai and her family, they had not escaped danger. Not long after her mother and siblings left for Canada, her husband, Ah Haw One, teaching athletics at the university in Wuhan, came under suspicion by the Red Guards. Universities, as institutions of culture, were centres for revolt, and every professor was scrutinized.

The head of his department, a well-known leader in academic circles and Ah One's mentor, had been persecuted for his former ties to the Kuomintang Party and sent into exile for re-education through hard labour. Ah One, as a colleague, was placed under house arrest in his dormitory at the university. For three months, he was investigated and his every action noted.

During his interrogations, he answered simply and honestly. He had never been interested in politics, nor in other matters having to do with the world in general, preferring to focus on the spiritual and inner forces of life. His questioners, cynical from the work they had been doing, tried to catch him in a lie, but it was impossible. Ah Lai had always described her husband as *jake*, straight—he was incapable of deception. Each day, the Red Guards watched him as he went about his teaching duties. During his private time, he exercised and practised qi gong, a meditation that focuses on the body's vital energy. He was working to perfect his own method of channelling his body's energy for healing.

While Ah Lai was able to visit him (her position at the military hospital in Donghu protected her from persecution), she did not learn of the specifics of his arrest until after his release. Having relatives on both sides of his family who lived in foreign countries had attracted suspicion, but records of Ah Dang's financial contributions to the Chinese Communist Party, and Ah Thloo's invitation to dine at the Great Hall of the People, might have helped exonerate Ah One. However, in the end, it was his prowess as a swimmer, his superb athleticism, and his abilities as a coach of successful teams that were the deciding factors.

Throughout the Cultural Revolution, people had emulated Mao's historic swim across the Yangtze River. Ah One was one of the most powerful swimmers in the country, and he had led the school's swim team at the annual reenactment as a tribute to Mao. The university needed him; the Red Guards dropped all the charges.

He also got a promotion. At the age of thirty-three, Guan Haw One became the head of the department of physical education, one of the youngest in China. From international competitions, his athletic teams brought back winning pennants that were proudly displayed in the university's gymnasium, and his school became famous for its athletic achievements. Most importantly, he completed thirteen crossings of the Yangtze River. Much later, he would be listed in the Who's Who of China's Qi Gong Masters.

Ah Lai of course wrote to her parents about Ah One's accomplishments, but she kept the secret of his dormitory arrest from them for thirty years. At first she was reluctant and afraid to write about it, as mail to foreign countries was subject to potential confiscation and review, and then, as time went on, life crowded the incident out of her immediate consciousness. But if her parents had known of the danger, would they have made more of an attempt to bring her family to Canada? Would she and her family have been allowed to leave the country? There were too many "what ifs" to contemplate. What was, was.

Left to right: Ah Lai holding Ah Thlam Moy, Ah One holding Ah Doon, and Ah Fuy, 1969.
PHOTOGRAPHER STUDIO, CHINA

In 1970, Canada established diplomatic relations with the People's Republic of China (PRC). A year later, as the PRC opened an embassy in Ottawa, and Canada sent its first delegation to China, the United Nations officially recognized the government. On October 11, 1973, Pierre Elliot Trudeau became the first Canadian prime minister to officially visit the PRC. Ah Dang and Ah Thloo preceded him.

In the spring of 1973, Ah Lai received a letter from her mother. Both of her parents were coming this time, with a plan to visit family in Hong Kong and Guangzhou before taking a tour of China. She and Ah One were invited to join them on the cross-country trip. She had not seen her father in a quarter-century; she was now thirty-six years old. She and Ah One had three children: Ah Bing Fuy was ten, Ah Bing Doon, a son, was six, and their younger daughter, Ah Thlam Moy, conceived after Ah One was released from arrest, was four. Though they still lived in Donghu, Ah Lai had been posted to work at the central hospital in Wuhan.

Ah Lai brought the whole family from Wuhan to Guangzhou to welcome her parents at the train station. It had been six years, but Ah Fuy's happy anticipation of a reunion with this grandmother set the tone for her siblings. Ah Dang picked up each grandchild to bestow a kiss. When he carried Ah Thlam Moy on his back, Ah Lai noticed the little girl snuggling up to him, obviously enjoying the aroma of his aftershave. At that time, aftershave and other personal care products, for either men or women, were rare commodities. The children stayed with Ah Thloo and Ah Dang at the Overseas Chinese Hotel, while Ah Lai and Ah One were again offered accommodations at uncle Ah Choo's apartment. Ah Dang ordered refreshments to be delivered to the room. The highlight for the children was drinking fizzy orange pop, available only to foreigners, through hollow reeds used as straws; it was a memorable treat.

The children were lavished with gifts, including a new girl's red bicycle (until then, they had all shared Ah Wei's old bicycle, still a sought-after commodity), a camera, a new radio with AM, FM, and short wave, and a tape recorder. Ah Dang had brought tapes so the family could learn English. When they returned to Wuhan, they did use the machine, but before they turned it on, they locked the doors. It was still dangerous to be seen, or heard, to be interested in things foreign.

Ah Ngange, who still lived with the family in Wuhan, was apparently pleased to see her adoptive son and daughter-in-law; throughout their stay, not a harsh word passed between them. Since 1967, Ah Ngange had been surrounded by her beloved granddaughter and great-grandchildren, and she had mellowed. In photographs with the children, she was actually smiling. She lived out the rest of her life in relative comfort, and in line with her reformed character, she was to die peacefully at home, in 1977.

o   o   o

Ah Thloo and Ah Dang had booked a fifteen-day trip to see the highlights of China. The tour started in Wuhan and included Zhengzhou, Beijing, Tianjin, Nanjing, Wuxi, Suzhou, Hangzhou, and Shanghai. They were to fly to most destinations, be picked up in a van each morning, and dropped off each night at the door of their hotel.

At first, Ah Lai and Ah One were denied tickets—the tour was considered too bourgeois for comrades of the state. Luckily for them, the Chinese

Ah One with his father and Ah Lai with both of
her parents at Beijing's Tiananmen Square, 1973.

tradition of "connections" had not been eliminated by the red flag of communism. The tour organizer had grown up in the same village as Ah One, and he remembered the now-famous athletic director. The couple was charged two hundred and twenty dollars per person, an exorbitant price, but it was happily paid by Ah Dang, and they became the first Chinese citizens to join the excursion. The operator was offered Ah Wei's old bicycle for the equivalent of around twenty-five dollars, for helping them.

Since the tour was designated for Overseas Chinese as a way to show off the country to nationals living in foreign countries, the amenities were first class. The clients had three meals a day and were treated to local specialties. At each stop, they toured the most famous landmarks. The highlights included the major sights in both Beijing and Shanghai, Mount Song and the Shaolin Temple in Zhengzhou, the thousand-year-old Dule Temple and the statue of Kuan Yin in Tianjin, and the Mausoleum of Dr. Sun Yat-sen in Nanjing.

In Wuxi on China's National Day, October 1, they were invited to dine with the mayor. For some reason, Ah Dang was considered an honoured guest and sat at the mayor's table, while Ah Lai and Ah Thloo sat together elsewhere. They were served the famous Wuxi Three Whites, a dish of white shrimp, whitebait, and whitefish.

Coincidentally, Ah One's father was visiting from the Kingdom of Brunei, in Southeast Asia, where he had lived and worked as a building contractor for decades. He had helped build the new palace for the king. He joined the tour at Beijing, but, already failing in health, he suffered a mild heart attack and had to be hospitalized. Ah One stayed behind to keep his father company—it had been many years since they had seen each other and they took advantage of the time to get reacquainted. The senior Guan recovered in time for them both to rejoin the tour in Shanghai. He had taken a chance in going to the People's Republic of China to see his son again; diplomatic relations between China and Brunei made it impossible for him to return to the country that he had called home. After the tour, when they all returned to Wuhan, he was reunited with his wife and lived with his family until his Chinese visa expired. Unable to extend the visa, he left for Hong Kong, where he had another heart attack and died, alone.

It had been important for Ah Lai to join the tour. Her father was going to be in China for only a short while, and she needed to spend as much of that time with him as possible. Twenty-five years earlier, she had been too young and too much in awe of him to try to get to know him. If she had been younger, her curiosity might have overcome her shyness, but she had been a teenager, herself changing too much to know how to cope with an unknown parent and authority figure. Now was the time to reconcile with her father. Earlier in her life, she had sought his approval by being frugal and a good student; it hadn't worked out as she had hoped. Now she was an adult, but she still needed affirmation as his daughter.

Ah Lai had imagined they would talk together—about his years in Canada and what he was doing now—and exchange views about modern China. She had expected he would ask her about her life and what she thought about things. Although she did not know how she would have responded, she used to dream that he would invite her to go to Canada. However, it was hard to

Ah Lai at work.

know what was on his mind, what he knew, how he felt. He was not a talk-ative man. She would have loved to know, but could not just ask, "What do you think of the life I have made?" or more importantly, "What do you think of me?"

Back in Wuhan, Ah Lai took her parents on a tour of the large, modern hospital where she worked as a department head. She noted with pride that the staff, including other doctors, greeted her and her parents with warmth and deference. Of course, acting as the interpreter, she was reluctant to fully translate her colleagues' enthusiastic compliments. Both parents just nodded and smiled; they asked few questions.

However, while Ah Lai's and Ah One's professional lives were satisfying, they had experienced very little economic gain. Everyone got the same wages, which were never enough to clothe and feed a household of four adults and three growing children. Much of the time, there were even more people, as

Ah Lai with her parents by a scenic lake, 1973.

poor relations from the village came to live with them, to help with the household chores and care for the children when Ah Lai was posted to different work places for months at a time.

What the tour guides neglected to show were the deprivations people faced during that time. In 1973, even without the Red Guards, the anarchy that was the Cultural Revolution was still going on. Its effects had spread to industry, agriculture, and even the country's finances. The shortages of consumer goods and food had become worse since 1966; lineups for staples were longer and the portions smaller.

Food was rationed with coupons. Each person got one kilo of meat per month. Fish was inexpensive, but to get fresh fish, one had to be in line by 3:00 AM. People held their places in line with a rock and hoped someone would kick it forward, or would ask a friend to pick up the fish for a tip, about the same amount as the fish itself. Ah Lai's family survived on legumes, tofu, and rice. She could remember every new piece of clothing she had had before 1985. The year her parents visited, Ah Lai was assigned a new apartment and additional food coupons in recognition of her foreign guests.

For the sake of her children, Ah Lai had to test the waters, hoping for a more permanent reunion with her parents. One evening, she screwed up her courage. "Father—could we go to Canada now? The children are getting older."

True to form, he responded bluntly, "Your situation looks good here. You are a doctor. It'd be different in Canada. Without English, you wouldn't be able to work as a doctor. Instead, you'd be doing *thlange foo gonge*, hard manual labour. You'd be better not to go."

Perhaps it was all true, but while the words were not harsh, the implications stung like nettles. Not wanting to argue with her father and spoil the short time they had together, Ah Lai said nothing more and let the matter drop.

Discussing it years later with her sister, Ah Lai would say, "When everyone is in the same situation, you don't feel bitter. We had it somewhat better than others; we'd have extra money from Father to buy a chicken or a fish. In comparison, we were much better off, wouldn't you say?"

o o o

In China, the 1970s remained politically turbulent. General Lin Biao, formerly named Mao's successor, attempted an armed coup d'état in 1971; it failed. In 1974, the Gang of Four, led by Mao's wife, Jiang Qing, seized power and imposed a two-year reign of terror that rivalled the worst of the Cultural Revolution.

When Premier Zhou Enlai died in January 1976, millions of citizens travelled to Tiananmen Square to lay wreaths, poems, and eulogies at the Monument to the People's Heroes. He had been the balanced face of the regime and the country mourned his loss deeply. Ah Thloo said a prayer out loud for Zhou Enlai's soul.

Not long afterwards, an earthquake measuring 8.2 on the Richter scale killed more than two hundred and forty-two thousand people in China. Some considered it a portent that the Mandate of Heaven was ending. Chairman Mao Zedong died in September 1976, his body embalmed and displayed in a crystal coffin in the Memorial Hall on Tiananmen Square. Ah Thloo, who was of the opinion that Chairman Mao had made it possible for China to become independent and proud, said a prayer out loud for his soul as well.

Grandma's Chinese name is Tue Sue. "Tue Sue" literally means autumn compassion. Autumn is the season of harvest and abundance. She was a rich woman of contentment because she appreciated and valued what she had and was gifted to find beauty in ordinary things. She once told me she was very lucky. "Who could have ever imagined a Chinese village girl like me would end up living in such a heavenly place?"

—Guan Binghui, *A Eulogy for Grandma*

FOURTEEN

A Cowherd in Paradise

AH DANG AND MICHAEL: VICTORIA, 1981

"Five hundred dollars? That was a fortune in 1921!" said Michael, Ah May's husband, of the head tax.

"Lotsa money, at dat time, can buy two house! But I have no leglets," Ah Dang replied in his heavily accented English.

"Aren't you angry at the government for making you pay to live in Canada?"

"At firs, I really mad. Sure. No one else have to pay. Jus Chinee. Not fair. Maybe govmen should say, 'Solly,' but I don't tink they will do dat, do you?"

"You're probably right. The government wouldn't apologize for something that happened so long ago." And Michael added sarcastically, "It has so many things to be sorry about."

When Ah Dang was asked what had drawn him to Canada, he explained, "Na-ting for me in China. In Canada, I find job, sometime very bad job, but in China, no work for no body. Too many war in China, all de time fighting!

They enjoyed it so much, they did it again—for the record! 1978
ROBERT WONG, MONTREAL

Canada peacefoo place. But I don't forget, I Chinee, my famly Chinee. I still love China. But now Canada my home."

After a long pause, he added, in a faraway voice, "One ting I leglet; my family in China so long without me. We no have chance to be family together. Dat why Ah May so plecious to me and to her mommy." He looked Michael straight in the eye. "I know you take good care my daughter."

○   ○   ○

AH DANG AND AH THLOO: MONTREAL AND VICTORIA, 1978–1984

This was a time of passages, both celebratory and mournful.

Ah Dang and Ah Thloo initiated the celebrations with a kiss. Not the dry, perfunctory, obligatory peck on the cheek he might have bestowed on her for her birthday or at New Year's, but a full-on, lip-to-lip, arms-embracing kiss. It was an intimate gesture, so spontaneously enacted in public that they both immediately burst into embarrassed laughter, each still clinging on to the other's arm. Ah Wei and Ah May, who witnessed this never-before-seen behaviour, were both so shocked and delighted that they demanded a repeat performance, so it could be recorded for posterity. Surprising everyone, including themselves, Ah Dang and Ah Thloo complied.

The couple had a wonderful reason for their antics; it was the day after Ah Wei's long-awaited wedding, in 1978, to Ah Sheung, his betrothed from China, after thirteen years of correspondence. As soon as Ah Sheung arrived in Montreal, Ah Wei took her on a holiday so they could get reacquainted. There were some things a man does not tell his mother to write to his fiancée.

Ah Thloo felt her prayers had been answered when Ah Sheung came back from her holiday with Ah Wei looking happy and content. For the first time in a long while, the look of uncertainty in her son's eyes had disappeared. The right girl had been chosen; her son would finally have someone to look after him and support him.

Their wedding was the biggest social event in Ah Dang's and Ah Thloo's lives. This was their opportunity to repay their social obligations after years of attendance at their friends' children's weddings. The whole church was invited, of course, and the dinner guest list read like the Who's Who of Chinatown society. Posing for the wedding pictures, Ah Thloo stood beside her son and held his hand, transmitting her joy and pride. The next day, when Ah Dang

Back, left to right: Ah Min, Ah Yee, Truman, Tina (Ah Yee's niece), and her husband. Middle, left to right: Anna and Helen. Front, left to right: Shannon (Ah Yee's youngest daughter), Ah May, Ah Sheung, Ah Wei, Ah Thloo, and Ah Dang, 1978.

UNKNOWN PHOTOGRAPHER, MONTREAL

had suddenly swept her into his arms and kissed her, she responded by kissing him back. She was jubilant!

A year later, Ah Dang had another opportunity to kiss his wife: in 1979, they marked a half-century of matrimony. While they had lived together for only a little over half that time, characterized more by discord than by harmony, they nevertheless marked the anniversary with a family celebration.

Looking back on their lives together, Ah Thloo was grateful for many things. Ah Dang had been faithful to her, he had provided for her and given her a good family life, and by bringing her to Canada, he had enabled her to learn about God's grace. Perhaps it was time to let go of the memory of the hurt inflicted on their wedding night, but a habit of fifty years was difficult to change.

Ah Thloo and Ah Dang on their 50th anniversary, 1979.
ROBERT WONG, MONTREAL

Ah Thloo recognized that Ah Dang was unique among men of his generation; he could overlook gender, despite a lifetime's association with traditional Chinese who maintained a preference for males. He had encouraged and supported all the females in their family to be educated, starting with herself. She was proud of him for that quality and she was content to be associated with him for it. So when the family posed for photos and the children asked Ah Thloo and Ah Dang for a kiss, she happily obliged.

Ah Dang and Ah Thloo had a complex relationship, for underneath their verbal clashes lay a mutual understanding of shared goals, grudging respect, and even love. Ah Dang kissed Ah Thloo for the gift of belonging. Between them, they had created a family, one he could call his own, that he would never abandon. They had both wanted a family and to give their children the opportunities they themselves had never had—an education, economic stability, and a safe place to live. With their daughters, they felt they had accomplished their task. Ah Wei had been, until his recent wedding, a source of constant concern, but worrying was the burden of parenting.

Ah Dang felt successful in other ways. Following in his adoptive father's footsteps, he had chosen Canada to be his home. He had come at a time when the Chinese were unwanted, but he and his countrymen had persevered against prejudice, and they were being accepted in the best institutions. His younger daughter had graduated from McGill University, one of the most renowned universities in the world, and they had celebrated in style at the restaurant at Place Ville Marie. He had reinvented himself from a discarded nobody to a businessman, and since his retirement in 1978, the government was supporting him with a pension.

In 1981, Ah Dang, Ah Thloo, Ah Wei, and his wife, Ah Sheung, all went to Victoria, British Columbia, where Ah May had been living and where she was getting married. At first Ah Dang had not been pleased to hear that Ah May's boyfriend was a white man. He and his wife had tried to instill in their daughter, throughout her life, the need to find a Chinese husband, but she hadn't cooperated, and Ah Thloo had been against an arranged marriage.

Ah May had met Michael Cockerell at the University of Guelph, in Ontario, where she was pursuing a master's degree in psychology and he was about to graduate as a veterinarian. She had brought the young man to the house in Montreal several times, and at her parents' golden anniversary dinner, Michael had done all the cleaning, even the pots and pans. Ah Thloo thought he and Ah May made a good team, but it was the caring way he treated Ah May that really endeared him to her. She noticed that Ah Dang always welcomed him to the house.

Ah Dang had also carefully observed both the way Michael treated Ah May, always solicitously, and his manners toward his elders, which were impeccable. He had certainly won over Ah Thloo. In fact, she had encouraged Ah May to move with Michael to Victoria, when he had found a job there right after his graduation. Ah Dang had agreed with his wife that it was better for Ah May to go there than to live in the dangerous city of Toronto by herself, even if she had to interrupt her studies. He just wished she hadn't moved so far.

On this trip, Ah Dang and Ah Thloo would stay for an extended visit; he had missed his daughter, and who knew when they would be able to see each other again? They flew straight to Victoria, where they finally met Michael's English parents; it was the beginning of a strong friendship.

Ah Thloo with Ah Wei and Michael in front of St. Evariste Street house, 1979.

After Ah Dang had done his duty by Ah May and given her life into the kind hands of her new husband, he could relax. Although he had not been back to Canada's West Coast since he left Vancouver by train in the early 1930s, he had no interest in visiting that city—he had few good recollections of the place. However, due to its proximity, the memories of those times came flooding back, and when Michael and Ah May asked questions about that stage of his life, he found himself talking about it.

He reminisced about living in small towns such as Salmo, being surrounded by trees so tall they blocked the sunlight; about catching salmon so big a single fish could feed a family; and about learning how to defend himself in a fist fight. Ah May remembered seeing his weapons in Montreal, but he hadn't brought them on this trip; in fact, he hadn't thought about them since his retirement. He told the young couple about the great gift his father's friend had given him, and about his train trip. "When I go Mon-de-haw, I take train tru Locky Moundan," he said. "Dis time when we come, fly oba—*oooy*, so big!" He had looked out the window the whole time the plane flew over the

Left to right: Doreen Cockerell, Ah Thloo, Ah Dang,
Jeff Cockerell, Ah May, and Michael, 1981.

ROBERT WONG, VICTORIA

mountains, grateful to finally see them, marvelling at their vastness and majesty, and searching for the railroad lines built by so many of his countrymen. He was surprised when Ah May asked him if he had worked on building the Canadian Pacific Railway. "I not so ole!" he laughed. The Last Spike had been driven many decades before he was even born, but he had worked on other railway lines in the interior of British Columbia.

When Ah Dang learned that Michael was also a naval officer and had sailed both coasts of Canada, he talked about the *Empress of Japan*, the once-famous ship he had arrived on, and about the voyage, but he couldn't bring himself to talk about what had happened when he first landed in Vancouver. He spoke about how his father had paid the five-hundred-dollar head tax, and when no one asked about the head tax receipt, he just kept quiet. Ah May and Michael did not have to know his whole life history.

Three months after the wedding, Ah Dang realized that he was losing his long-time fight with diabetes. His body was betraying him. He did not want to burden Ah May with his care or have her worry about him, arguing with him about what he could or couldn't eat or do; he did not want her to watch him deteriorate and die. He left Ah May with one last request, to be undertaken after his death and then, reluctantly, he and Ah Thloo went home.

Ah Dang's condition deteriorated after their return to Montreal. A series of small strokes left him unresponsive, except at meal times, when he became animated and anxious to feed his ironically healthy appetite. The self-made man had disappeared. He was now in his eighth decade and all his life he had fought hard for his achievements; perhaps he was tired of fighting. His pride was what had made him succeed in a hostile world; perhaps his pride required him to disengage from a body that was failing. There were only a few things he could now control and he seemed to have relinquished everything else.

Ah Dang died December 23, 1983. As was traditional in the Chinese culture, the family booked the funeral home for several days, for the wake, visitations, and final service. His body was laid out in an open casket, and a large framed photograph of him was displayed on a small table near his head. People would go up to the casket, kowtow three times, perhaps give him a pat or say a few words, then meet with the family and others who had come to pay their respects.

Ah Dang's passing enabled Ah Thloo to soften her carapace of anger. She spent long moments standing beside him, touching him and praying for his soul. She responded with gratitude to visitors. Her tears were close to the surface, but they flowed quietly and with dignity.

Ah Wei wore his emotions on his sleeve, but Ah Thloo noted with pride that he rose to the task of becoming the head of the family, welcoming visitors and chatting with everyone who came, making them feel at ease. Ah May came from Victoria by herself; Michael couldn't leave his new solo practice. She mourned her father quietly. Ah Sheung was the most demonstrative mourner; she wailed, wept, and prostrated herself on the floor, until Ah Wei helped her up.

Some of the Canadian-born visitors looked embarrassed, but the elders realized that if the funeral had been held in China, the family would have hired professional mourners to loudly show what a good person the deceased had been. With her lamentations, Ah Sheung was following tradition. She had become close to Ah Dang, and during his final years, she had been his caregiver. When Ah Dang would not listen to his wife or his son, Ah Sheung could coax him into doing whatever was required. She mourned him now like a loyal daughter-in-law.

Each day, more wreaths and flower arrangements were placed around Ah Dang. Ah Lai and Ah One, and other family members in China, sent money to buy special bouquets. Attached to each arrangement were red silk ribbons, adorned with black Chinese calligraphy expressing condolences and wishes for a safe journey to heaven. Beautiful and numerous, they testified to Ah Dang's esteemed position in the community.

Ah Thloo drank tea, ate cookies, and shared stories. She even laughed. Her niece, Ah Yee, came with her husband and their older children and they reminisced about the times they had spent together. Many of Ah Dang's old friends came—it was good to hear how much he had been respected in the Chinatown community. He would have been proud to see how many people attended both his funeral service and the memorial banquet later.

White is the colour of traditional Chinese mourning, but the family chose to wear dark colours, with white armbands. It was also the custom to burn all the clothing worn for the funeral, to dissipate bad luck, but no one could bear to part with the mementos of that time. Family members were instructed not to cut or wash their hair until after the funeral.

When the family went back home after the service, to rest before attending the memorial dinner in Chinatown, Ah Thloo's friends from church were already there. Over the past few days, the ladies had taken turns going to pay their respects, then returned to scour Ah Dang's room clean, cover all the mirrors and glass surfaces, cook meals, and console Ah Thloo and her relatives with prayers, hugs, and food. After the funeral, they greeted the family with small sprigs of fresh, fragrant cedar to pin to their clothes and gave each of them a candy to eat immediately. They had filled special red envelopes with a piece of candy and a dollar bill, to be handed out to each of the dinner guests. The candy was to be consumed to bring sweetness back to life and the money was to be spent; keeping it would have brought bad luck. Though they were all Christians, some customs were hard to break.

Ah Dang's body was cremated and as he had requested, also contrary to Chinese convention, Ah May took his ashes to Victoria. There, she and Michael performed a simple ceremony over the ocean, releasing his earthly particles to the wind and sea. Ah Dang now wanders the world wherever,

Portrait of Guey Dang Wong, 1960s.
JASPER TANG, MONTREAL

whenever, and for however long his spirit chooses. No more discriminating laws, no more closed borders, no more disabilities can limit him.

o   o   o

AH THLOO AND AH LAI: CHINA, 1985

With widowhood came freedom for Ah Thloo, and in 1985, she returned to China for a long visit. Not wanting to be bound by an artificial timeline, she bought a one-way ticket to visit her extended family one last time.

Ah Lai and her family then lived in Guangzhou, where she headed the department of internal medicine. She had also completed training in traditional Chinese medicine and had joined her husband, Ah One, in his growing practice as a qi gong master healer. Together, they treated illnesses and relieved chronic pain for patients who came from around the world to see them.

Ah Thloo, at seventy-four, was still curious about the world and open to new experiences. She learned qi gong and was a diligent practitioner. Ah One included her in his healing circles, adding her qi, vital energy, to the process when dealing with clients. She was also still eager to travel and Ah Lai made a point of taking her mother to visit new places. They had time to talk and to reminisce, and they became friends.

Ah Lai's eldest daughter, Ah Fuy, had received permission from the United States immigration department to undertake postgraduate studies in medical administration. The commotion and the festive air of opportunity that had accompanied her success was now tinged with uncertainty and anxiety for her safety in faraway America. The best way to protect her, Ah Lai reasoned, would be to join her there.

Also, Ah One was broadening his reputation as a healer and the fees they received added to their income. Together, they made a good team; they would be able to establish a practice wherever there was a large Chinese community and make a good living. She *had* to ask her mother to help her emigrate. It was like asking for a favour, and in her lifetime, she had not asked much of her parents.

"Ah Ma, the children are growing up," said Ah Lai.

"Yes, how lucky you are. They're studious and obedient. You've raised them well."

Left to right: A cousin, Ah Min, Ah Yee, Tew May Mah (Ah Yee's mother and Ah Thloo's second sister), Ah Choo (Ah Thloo's younger brother), 1985.
TRUMAN WONG, CHINA

"Ah Ma, do you remember Ah Yea's papers?"

With a clenched stomach, Ah Thloo knew where the conversation was leading and before Ah Lai could ask her anything else, she told her daughter the bad news. "Ah Nui, your . . . your papers have been given away." She stumbled at first, and it took all her courage to look her daughter in the eye as she told the full story. She did not lay the blame on her husband; they had agreed at the time it was the right thing to do.

When her daughter said nothing, she continued. "If we go back and apply for you now, the government will know that the Wong Lai Quen who came to Canada before you was a fake. Our whole family might be deported."

This bombshell naturally frightened Ah Lai; she did not want to jeopardize the security of her family in Canada. She had to set aside her dreams once again. Despite what her mother had said about it having been a mutual decision, a bitter thought came into her mind: *Ah Yea has let me down once more.*

○   ○   ○

AH THLOO AND AH MAY: VICTORIA, 1986–2002

Ah Thloo arrived back from China in time to witness Ah May's graduation from the University of Victoria. Ah May had fulfilled a promise she had made seven years previously, when she left the University of Guelph prematurely, to complete a postgraduate degree, this time in public administration. While Ah Thloo was visiting Michael and Ah May, she accepted their invitation to live with them. In Montreal, she had been sharing the duplex with Ah Wei and his wife, but it was time to get away from the long, frigid winters and hot, humid summers. Ah Thloo thankfully acknowledged how generous and unusual it was for a non-Chinese man, raised in the Western tradition of independence, to invite his mother-in-law to live with him.

Ah Thloo and Ah May had lived apart for only eight years. While Ah Thloo had not been as demonstrative as Ah Dang with their daughter, she had always felt a deep attachment to this "last girl" and knew that the feeling was returned. But it was not until 1993, when Ah May called her back from a three-day diabetic coma, that their bond became invincible. Ah Thloo couldn't recall how it had transpired, but she did remember waking up in a hospital one day, responding to her daughter's question, "Mommy, do you know who I am?" with the obvious answer, "You are my *thlem goyne*, my heart-liver and my core. You are Ah May."

The relationship between Ah Thloo, Ah May, and Michael was easy and warm. Ah Thloo insisted on taking over cooking the evening meals from Ah May. She planted and tended the garden and proudly consumed the harvests. She travelled with them, all the while keeping her eyes open to take in the passing sights. When Michael's parents, Jeff and Doreen Cockerell, moved to a house next door, Ah Thloo started playing mah-jong again. She was eighty-one and the last time she had played was when she was eighteen. Although Ah Thloo spoke very little English and they did not speak any Chinese, the three of them became close.

"Sixo-calack. You come," Ah Thloo would call to say in her pidgin English. That was the Cockerells' invitation for dinner at six o'clock and a game of mah-jong, at which Ah May would be the fourth. They played three times a week, for hotly contested pennies a point. The winner kept half the pot, while the pot bought a monthly treat for dinner.

Ah Wei died in 2001, of a stroke, at the too-young age of fifty-three. All the family's bad genes had apparently been visited upon him, shortening his life. One of the most difficult things for a mother to bear is the death of a child, no

Ah Thloo proudly displays her garden harvest, 1989.

Ah Thloo plays Mah Jong with in-laws Doreen and Jeff and
goddaughter Ah Ngan Jean (visiting from Hong Kong), 1990s.
MAY Q. WONG, VICTORIA

matter how old that child is. Ah Thloo had worried about Ah Wei all his
life; he had been needier than her other two children. As he grew older,
everything was a struggle for him—mentally, socially, and physically. At the
evening meals, her prayers for him were the longest and most fervent. Ah
Thloo absorbed the sad news philosophically; she was relieved that he no
longer had to battle his demons. She sent Ah May and Michael to Montreal,
to give Ah Wei's eulogy and to bestow one last kiss from her.

About three times a year, Ah May took her mother on the ferry to
Vancouver, to visit friends and to shop. Ah Thloo became reacquainted with
Ah Aie, the little girl who had slept in her house in the hamlet. Ah Aie had
married a Gim San law who worked in the fishing camps in remote parts
of British Columbia. Now a senior herself, she and her family had lived in
Vancouver for many years.

It was through their stories about life in the hamlet that Ah May finally
understood Ah Aie's relationship with the Wong family. She, Ah Lien, and
their older sister, Ah Ngan, who lived in Los Angeles and loved to gamble,

were the daughters of Ah Ngay Gonge, the man who had given Ah Dang the train ticket to Montreal; he was the old man Ah May and her brother used to visit at his laundry on St. Hubert Street when she was very young. Sadly, only the middle daughter, Ah Lien, ever saw their father after he went to Montreal. The eldest was married and had moved away by the time he went back to China to father the youngest. After Ah Thloo married and left the hamlet, she never saw Ah Lien again, but they kept in touch through letters.

Ah Aie and Ah Ngan came together to Victoria to visit Ah Thloo. They had different personalities and had lived very different lives, but when they were all together, they giggled like little girls. They sat close, with Ah Thloo between them, holding hands, as if they could not bear to lose one another. They reminisced about *giew see*, olden times, laughing about how poor they had been, and what they had had to do to make do.

"I am so lucky! How was I so fortunate as to have this last daughter, and live out my life in this paradise on earth?" Ah Thloo wondered out loud to her friends, as they gazed at the mature trees framing a view of the ocean, with mountains a distant backdrop. "The weather is so good, the air is clean, and it is never too hot, like *nonge toon* or too cold like Mon-de-haw. When I was a girl, watching our buffalo, I never dreamed of coming to live in a place like this."

All of Ah Thloo's "children" came to visit her. Her goddaughter, Ah Ngan Jean, brought her physician husband and daughters, Susan and Susanna, from Hong Kong. The girls came back to visit Ah Thloo four years later, to introduce Susan's fiancé to their surrogate grandmother. The girls could not speak directly to Ah Thloo—they spoke Cantonese and did not understand her dialect, so they spoke English to Ah May, who translated—but they all felt a special bond.

Ah Sang, the young man who had taken Ah Thloo and young Ah Wei touring in Hong Kong while they waited for their visas, travelled from Australia to visit. He and his son Alan were on a round-the-world trip and made a point of stopping in Victoria.

All three of Ah Lai's children came to see their grandmother. Ah Fuy, the eldest, visited a number of times from New York, while Ah Thlam Moy, the youngest, came from Australia. Ah Doon moved to Victoria from China with his wife.

Ah Thloo sitting between Ah Aie and Ah Ngan, 1990s.
MAY Q. WONG, VICTORIA

Ah Fuy and Ah Thloo had built a bond since 1966, when the girl was only three years old, and the relationship had deepened through her earlier trips to Montreal from New York. During one of her visits to Victoria, when Ah May was away with Michael, Ah Thloo shared the story of her wedding night and the events that had started the rift between Ah Dang and herself. She had never told the story to anyone, but it was time someone else knew what had happened. The simple act of telling it made Ah Thloo feel like a swan's feather being lifted by a fresh spring breeze toward the heavens; she could see so far that her perspective was different. The memory stayed, but the last vestiges of her resentment and hurt were gone, replaced by a feeling of peace. Afterwards, grandmother and granddaughter cried, and as they dried each other's tears, they both recognized the change in Ah Thloo. Thereafter, Ah Thloo could even acknowledge her own love for Ah Dang.

Ah Sang and son Alan bring an Australian sheep skin for Ah Thloo, 1990s.

Ah Lai eventually came to Canada as well, and she and Ah One lived in Ah May and Michael's house on three separate occasions, varying in duration from six months to a year, between 1994 and 1999. Michael learned to speak Ah Thloo's Chinese dialect and Ah One taught everyone qi gong. An inventive and accomplished cook, Ah Lai offered her culinary skills as a gift and eventually pursuaded her mother to relinquish the kitchen. In 2002, they emigrated to Canada, sponsored by their son. Ah Lai no longer needed her father's papers.

Ah Thloo lived with Michael and Ah May for more than fifteen years. "In all that time, we never had a cross word between us," Michael liked to say of his relationship with his mother-in-law. "She respected our boundaries, never interfered, and never took sides." It was not that Michael and Ah Thloo didn't understand each other; rather, that they had a special rapport that did not always require language. Neither Ah May nor Michael had any idea how much English Ah Thloo actually understood, but she would sometimes surprise them by commenting appropriately, in Chinese, about a topic they were discussing. However, if they argued, Ah Thloo just quietly went to her

Left to right: Ah Fuy, Ah Lai, Ah Thloo, and Ah May
sitting in front of the heavenly view, 1990s.
RON OF TIVOLI STUDIOS, VICTORIA

room and left them alone to resolve their problems. If Ah May talked to her about it, she comforted her daughter but never said anything against "Mikoo." Ah Thloo's own marriage had taught her that issues between a husband and wife could not be resolved by anyone else.

Before Ah May moved in with Michael, Ah Thloo had predicted, "He will take good care of you." Had she known he would take that same care with her? His care, and her acceptance of that care, were a reflection of their mutual love and respect. There is a special grace in allowing oneself to be cared for. Ah Thloo was always thankful; she also kept her sense of humour.

Ah May had been raised to expect to be an active caregiver for her aging parents. She felt she had received from them everything a person needed to succeed in life—love, a sense of humour, and trust—and she had accepted her caregiving role as a privilege. Now she could give back.

One of the things Ah May did for her mother was a pedicure, which was a bonding ritual for them. Ah Thloo often reminisced about the routine she had developed as a girl with her dear grandmother, and she took obvious pleasure from having her feet and toes touched, manipulated, and kneaded. As a child, Ah May had always been disappointed when she couldn't get a laugh from her mother by tickling her feet. "It's from walking barefoot for half of my life. A farmer's daughter can't survive in the rice fields with sensitive, thin-skinned feet. Every day I stood in water and my toes kept me balanced in the mud," Ah Thloo noted practically, as Ah May gave her a massage.

Ah Thloo would sit back and tell Ah May stories about giew see, the olden times. One day Ah May asked her about Canada's old immigration laws, as she had recently found her father's head tax receipt. It was folded up in an old, blue, plastic bank account book holder. It looked well worn: the folds were reinforced with tape, it had yellowed with age, and it smelled old and bitter.

It must have been a precious thing—it was her father's passport to a new life, his entry fee to a wonderland full of promise, his key to the door of fulfillment—but he had never talked to Ah May about the how doo, head tax. It wasn't a secret; it just wasn't something the family talked about. Since her childhood, Ah May had known about the tax and the law that had resulted in estranged families like hers.

It wasn't until her mother told Ah May about Ah Dang's early life that she could guess at why her father had kept the paper hidden. Perhaps the document served as a symbol of his own dark experiences in those long ago days. It was also a shameful testimonial to the way Canada had targeted the Chinese people for discrimination. No other immigrant group had been shut out entirely, forcing a generation of men to endure a lifetime away from their families.

Despite the discrimination Ah Dang had been subjected to, he was a proud Canadian. He took his rights and responsibilities as a citizen seriously, paid his taxes, and happily showed off his Canadian passport whenever he

The Guan family gathers to celebrate a birthday, 1995.
A GODDAUGHTER, GUANGZHOU

travelled abroad. He could have thrown away the painful record when it was no longer required as identification, but in addition to the sorrow it was drenched in, perhaps it was also a reminder of his adoptive father's trust: that he might reinvent himself and create a life filled with more hope than bitterness.

On a day when Ah May was giving her mother a pedicure, a radio program featured a Chinese-Canadian organization that was lobbying for restitution. The speaker was asking people who had paid the tax, or were direct relatives of those who had paid it, to make themselves and their views on compensation known. Conversing in Chinese, Ah May asked her mother what she thought. "Mommy, a Chinese group is asking the government for redress on the head tax."

"What are they asking for?"

"An apology and a symbolic repayment of the head tax."

"An apology is a good idea. We Chinese built the railroad that helped make Canada a country. There was no reason to tax new immigrants after we finished the job. When the tax didn't work, they stopped us all from coming. That's why your father lived here and I had to stay in China for so long after we were married."

"Did he have enough money to bring you here?"

"Sure, he had money. Your father worked hard and saved enough to go back to China three times. We would have been safer in Canada. Remember, there were wars all over China. But Canada wouldn't let our family come. The government has to say, 'I am sorry for discriminating against the Chinese.'"

"What about paying back the five hundred dollars Daddy paid?"

"How much would be enough? Some of it? All of it? Would they give interest, or give today's value? Too little would be insulting. How much would be too much? Someone is bound to complain, no matter what the amount. No amount they give could make me forget the starvation and fear we endured by being left behind. Nothing would erase the heartache of separation between your father and your sister and brother. Gan-na-aie is known as a fair country. That's why so many people from around the world come here to live. To keep being fair, Gan-na-aie must recognize its wrongs and apologize."

Unfortunately, Ah Thloo missed the apology by four years.

However, she lived to witness the return of Hong Kong to the People's Republic of China, and more importantly, she was reunited with her daughter, Ah Lai, in Canada, and met all three of her great-granddaughters. Her last words were about how clever those girls had become and much she loved her family.

On December 14, 2002, the pastor from the Chinese church joined Ah Thloo's family by her bedside. It was as if Ah Thloo had been waiting for a formal introduction to heaven, for as soon as the pastor began to pray, she shrugged off her frail earthly mantle and passed away peacefully.

Her daughters made sure Ah Thloo took her final journey fully clothed, complete with shoes, underwear, a pantsuit, and a new Christmas vest. She would have enjoyed her funeral banquet, attended by many friends from the church and the community. Her cremated remains are contained in a cloisonné, Chinese-style urn, for she did not want her ashes to be scattered. They rest instead with a view of the heavenly landscape she enjoyed so much in life.

Portrait of Jang Tue Sue Wong, 1970s.
ROBERT WONG, MONTREAL

My dear fellow citizen: Today you are becoming a member of our great Canadian family, with its common values of freedom, respect, tolerance and sharing. By coming here, you have enriched our collective history with your own experience.

—Governor General Michaëlle Jean, Letter to New Citizens

Canadian—At Last

◯

VICTORIA, 2007

"I swear that I will be faithful . . ."

With my nephew, Ah Doon, translating for his parents, Ah Lai and Ah One repeated the phrases in Chinese. This was the final step in becoming Canadian citizens; their required five years of residency had passed in a flash, and they had submitted their applications only a few months earlier. Their English was still far from fluent, coming to Canada as they had in their sixties. Learning a new language was hard, so they were given some leeway with the translation. In addition, the officials had come to their home to perform the ceremony, all quite a sharp contrast to the drawn-out process experienced by our father when he had sought a country to belong to.

Judge Brown, a citizenship judge based in Vancouver, came to Ah Lai and Ah One's apartment in Victoria on June 13, 2007, to conduct a private swearing-in, in deference to Ah One's bedridden condition. He was blind, and his right side was partially paralyzed, the result of a long-ago stroke, so he raised his left hand during the ceremony. Michael and I took the pictures for posterity.

Donning her black robe, accented with pink, Judge Brown opened the formal ceremony with a talk about the significance of becoming citizens during the year 2007. "Canada is celebrating sixty years of Canadian citizenship. Before 1947, people were considered British citizens. The Canadian Citizenship Act recognized a separate Canadian identity from the rest of Great Britain."

That year was also when the Chinese Immigration Act of 1923, known as the Chinese Exclusion Act, was finally repealed, lifting the ban on Chinese immigration. On June 22, 2006, Prime Minister Stephen Harper apologized, on behalf of Canada, for discriminating against the Chinese by imposing a head tax.

While neither of my parents lived to witness the apology, they would have approved of the government's acknowledging this institutionalized prejudice and been satisfied that it was done formally, in the House of Commons, where the original offending legislation had been passed. Mother and Father had lived their lives in Canada with their heads held high, not allowing other people's attitudes and behaviours to cow them. They were as proud of their Chinese heritage as they were of their Canadian identities, and they had patiently hoped that the Canadian government, with its reputation for upholding justice, would eventually right this particular wrong.

About a year after the prime minister's announcement, I requested a copy of the apology statement to keep with my father's head tax document. I had not known the date of my sister's citizenship appointment when I made the call, but when the statement arrived on the very morning of the ceremony, it seemed fitting that she, as the one who had stayed in China because of the legislation, should be presented with it.

My sister and brother-in-law were among the one hundred and sixty thousand new citizens sworn in that year. Eighty-five percent of all immigrants to this country want to be Canadians. And why not? Canada now revels in its diversity.

The judge kept her message brief, then started the recitation of the Oath of Allegiance, pausing after each phrase. My sister held a copy of the oath in her free hand and stood close to Ah One's raised hospital bed. Ah Doon stood between his parents, translating. All three started with slight smiles on their faces. As they came to the end, their smiles and voices, especially my

Ah One, Ah Lai, and Ah Thloo enjoy a famous garden, 1990s.
MAY Q. WONG, VICTORIA

brother-in-law's, became wider and stronger, emphasizing each phrase with anticipation of their new status. ". . . and bear true allegiance to Her Majesty Queen Elizabeth the Second, Queen of Canada, . . . and that I will faithfully observe the laws of Canada and fulfil my duties as a Canadian citizen."

Then Ah One turned his beaming face toward our voices to pose for a photograph. Written messages from Governor General Michaëlle Jean and from the minister of citizenship and immigration were also presented.

"Congratulations!" said Judge Brown, shaking their hands. "I welcome you as Canadian citizens!"

Author with her father, 1981.
ROBERT WONG, VICTORIA

By taking on the mantle of Canadian citizenship, my sister not only shed her Chinese passport but also shrugged off the stigma of being the daughter left behind. She had accepted the apology by Canada's highest office as well as the challenge of creating a new life in her parents' chosen country.

Michael and I rushed forward to hug Ah Lai and her husband. Returning my welcoming embrace, my sister said, with a smile and a catch in her voice, "Ah Moy, Mommy and Daddy in heaven are very happy. Today, we have realized their lifelong dream. Finally, our whole family has been reunited as Canadians!"

Author with her mother, portrait taken to commemorate the
centenary of the Victoria Chinese Presbyterian Church, 1992.

Glossary

May's Phonetic Hoyping	English	Pinyin
aie foo	underwear	nei yi ku
aiyahh or aiya	an expression of surprise, frustration or pain	ai ya
chan taw	to weed	chu cao
choot tae	a type of tae with a soft pouch made from sticky rice flour with a sugar filling	tian de nuo mi dian xin
choot ngiet gat how	one month haircutting ceremony	ti man yue ying er qu ming, ti tou de yi shi
daaw	cooking hearth	zao tai
day moy	sisters, sworn sisters, girl friend	jie mei
dim sum	small savoury and/or sweet cakes	dian xin
donge	a type of dim sum wrapped in bamboo leaves, tied with twine and boiled	zong zi
faan	cooked rice	mi fan
fa haang	flowered hair dressing	hua de tou shi
fat gaw	delicately sweetened steamed cake	tian de gao dian
foo	bitter suffering	ku
ga hieng	a family and a home	jia xiang
gai fong	liberation, referring to the communist revolution	lin ju
gai longe	a type of tae with a crunchy pouch made from sticky rice flour filled with savoury stuffing	hua sheng xian de nuo mi dian xin
giew see	olden times	yi qian
gim ja toy	dried lily stalks	jin zhen cai
gim san	gold Mountain, referring to Canada or United States	jin shan
gim san law	gold mountain man	qu jin shan de ren
gong goo-doy	speaking stories (literally) or telling stories	jiang gu shi

May's Phonetic Hoyping	English	Pinyin
guey law	devil or ghost men or hooligans—also an uncomplimentary phrase for white men	lao wai
gwoh nien	new year's festival	xin nian
haam ha	fermented shrimp paste	xian xia jiang
haam nguey	dried salted fish	xian yu
haam toy	pickled vegetables	xian cai
hai ngow nui	cowherd girl	kan niu de nu hai
haw taw	gather or rake hay	ba cao
hiang aie or hiang	common room or living room	ke ting
hiang wa	to listen to being told or to be obedient	ting hua
hiem wa	sweet words	tian yan mi yu
hong ngange	Chinese people	zhong guo ren
hong ngange gai	Chinatown	tang ren jie
hoo mien	saving face	yao mian zi
how doo	head Tax	ren tou shui
jake	straight (literally) or honest	cheng shi/zheng zhi
jat giek	bound feet	guo jiao
jook	savoury rice porridge	xi fan/zhou
kai ma	god-mother	gan ma
kange nang woo joit	study hard, avoid stupidity	jiang qin bu zhuo
kien lake	strength	qin lao
kong jien	war of resistance against Japan	kang zhan
kowtow	performing low bows of respect	ke tou
lai gim	bride price	pin li/li jin
lap ap	cured duck	na ya
lap cheong	cured Chinese sausage	na chang
lap ngoke	cured pork belly	na rou

May's Phonetic Hoyping	English	Pinyin
law nai	coils of caked dirt and old skin	zhi wu gou
law nui	old maid	nian ji da de dan shen nü ren
liak	intelligent or clever	cong min de ling li
lieng giew	sedan chair	jiao zi
lie see	money wrapped in red paper	li shi/ya sui qian
lok aye	touching the ground	zhan zai di shang
man how	steamed bread rolls	man tou
maange foon	blind wedding	mang hun ya jia
mak see	writing out from memory	mo shu
m'loy, m'heuy	weren't coming or going	bu lai bu qu
mai	raw rice	mi
moi ngange	matchmaker	mei po
moin how	front door	men kou/qian men
nat gok	pre-wedding gathering like a bridal shower	ni ge
ngai	ants	ma yi
ngang giang	stiff necked (literally) or stubborn	jue jiang, wan gu
nguey chee gaang	shark fin soup	yu chi geng
niem see	memorize text	bei shu
nonge toon	rural hamlet	nong cun
nui ngange	female person or woman	nü ren
nui oak	girls' house	nü hai de jia
oo deah	many thanks or thank you	xie xie
sui thlem	gift to host	shou xin
tange fong	living conditions	qing kuang
thlai ngange	Western people or white people	xin fang ren
thlange foo gonge	hard manual labour	xin ku de gong zuo
thlange saang	teacher	lao shi
thlay	four or dead	si
thlem goyn	heart-liver or core or dearest	xin gan bao bei

May's Phonetic Hoyping	English	Pinyin
thlem tiek	with a hurting heart	xin teng
thliew jiang	folding privacy screen	ping zhang
thloo muun	sophisticated	si wen
thlonge	any accompaniment for rice	fan cai
tien	cash or coins or money	qian
via aie	a cloth baby sling	ying er bei dai
wa kiew	overseas Chinese	hai wai hua ren
war siew guy	stuffed crispy chicken	shao quan ji
yen waw gaang	bird's nest soup	yan wo geng
yuon	round or a type of dumpling	yuan

Bibliography

Books and Articles

Aiken, Rebecca B. *Montreal Chinese Property Ownership and Occupational Change, 1881–1981*. New York: AMS Press, Inc., 1989.

Bray, Francesca. *The Rice Economies: Technology and Development in Asian Societies*. Oxford: Basil Blackwell Ltd., 1986.

Buchanan, Keith McPherson, et al. *China*. New York: Crown, 1980.

Chan, Kwok Bun. *Smoke and Fire: The Chinese in Montreal*. Hong Kong: The Chinese University Press, 1991.

Chinese Academy of Social Sciences. *Information China: The Comprehensive and Authoritative Reference Source of New China*, Volume 1. Oxford: Pergamon Press, 1989.

Con, Harry, Ronald J. Con, Graham Johnson, Edgar Wickberg, and William E. Willmott, edited by Edgar Wickberg. "From China to Canada: A History of the Chinese Communities in Canada." In *Generations: A History of Canada's Peoples*. Toronto: McClelland & Stewart Ltd. in association with Multiculturalism Directorate, Department of the Secretary of State and Supply and Services Canada, 1982.

Eastman, Lloyd E. *Family Fields and Ancestors: Constancy and Change in China's Social and Economic History, 1550–1949*. New York: Oxford University Press, 1988.

Ebrey, Patricia Buckley. *Cambridge Illustrated History of China*. New York: Cambridge University Press, 1996.

Economic Research Bureau of City of Montreal. *Abridged History of Montreal*. Montreal: Economic Research Bureau of City of Montreal, 1970.

Fairbank, John King. *The Great Chinese Revolution, 1800–1985*. New York: Harper & Row, Publishers, 1986.

———. *China: A New History*. Cambridge, MA: Belknap Press of Harvard University Press, 1992.

Fenby, Jonathan. *The Penguin History of Modern China: The Fall and Rise of a Great Power, 1850–2008*. London: Allen Lane, 2008.

Fields, Adele. "The First Days of Marriage." In *Chinese Women: A Thousand Pieces of Gold: An Anthology*, selected and edited by Barbara-Sue White. New York: Oxford University Press, 2003.

Foreign Languages Press. *Peking: A Tourist Guide*. Peking: Foreign Languages Press, 1960.

Gubbay, Aline. *Montreal: The Mountain and the River*. Translated by Rachel Levy. Montreal: Trillium Books, 1981.

Helly, Denise. *Les Chinois a Montreal (1877–1951)*. Quebec: Institut quebecois de recherché sur la culture, 1987.

Hillel, Edward. *The Main: Portrait of a Neighbourhood.* Toronto: Key Porter Books, 1987.

Hoe, Ban Seng. *Beyond the Golden Mountain.* Hull, PQ: Canadian Museum of Civilization, 1989.

Hsia, H. J. "Marriage Through Six Rituals." In *The Fair Sex in China: They Lift Up Half the Sky*, edited by H.J. Hsia. Albuquerque, NM: American Association Publishers, 1992.

Jaschok, Maria, and Suzanne Miers, editors. *Women and Chinese Patriarchy: Submission, Servitude, and Escape.* Hong Kong: Hong Kong University Press, 1994.

Lai, David Chuenyan. *Chinatown: Towns Within Cities in Canada.* Vancouver: University of British Columbia Press, 1988.

Li, Peter S. *Chinese in Canada.* Toronto: Oxford University Press, 1998.

MacFarquhar, Roderick, and John K. Fairbank, editors. *The People's Republic, Part 2: Revolutions Within the Chinese Revolution, 1966–1982*, Volume 15. *The Cambridge History of China.* Fairbank, John K., and Denis Twitchett, general editors. Cambridge: Cambridge University Press, 1992

Ng, Wing Chung. *The Chinese in Vancouver (1945–80): The Pursuit of Identity and Power.* Vancouver: University of British Columbia Press, 2000.

Ni, Hua-Ching. *Tao: The Subtle Universal Law and the Integral Way of Life*, second edition. Santa Monica, CA: Seven Star Communications, 1979.

Pomelo, Walter Keoki Quan. "Leaving China: A Brief History of Emigration." In *Being Chinese: Voices from the Diaspora*, edited by Wei Djao. Tucson, AZ: University of Arizona Press, 2003.

Prevost, Robert. *Montreal: A History.* Translated by Elizabeth Meuller and Robert Chodos. Toronto: McClelland & Stewart, 1993.

Shifeng, Zheng. *China: All Provinces and Autonomous Regions.* New York: McGraw-Hill, 1980.

Sievers, Sharon. "Women in China, Japan and Korea." In *Women in Asia: Restoring Women to History*, edited by Barbara N. Remusack and Sharon Sievers. Bloomington, IN: Indiana University Press, 1999.

Skeldon, Ronald. "The Chinese Diaspora or the Migration of Chinese Peoples?" In *The Chinese Diaspora: Space, Place, Mobility and Identity*, edited by Laurence J.C. Ma and Carolyn Cartier. Lanham, MD: Rowman and Littlefield Publishers, Inc., 2003.

Tan, Thomas su-wee. *Your Chinese Roots: The Overseas Chinese Story.* Union City, CA: Heian International, Inc., 1987.

Taylor, Charles. "The Chinese Never Kiss." In *Chinese Women: A Thousand Pieces of Gold: An Anthology*, selected and edited by Barbara-Sue White. New York: Oxford University Press, 2003.

Turner, Robert D. *The Pacific Empresses: An Illustrated History of Canadian Pacific Railway's Empress Liners on the Pacific Ocean.* Victoria: Sono Nis Press, 1981.

Wallace, W. Stewart, general editor. *Encyclopaedia of Canada.* Toronto: University Associates of Canada, Ltd., 1948.

Yee, Paul. *Struggle and Hope: The Story of Chinese Canadians.* Toronto: Umbrella Press, 1996.

———. *Chinatown: An Illustrated History of the Chinese Communities of Victoria, Vancouver, Calgary, Winnipeg, Toronto, Ottawa, Montreal, and Halifax.* Toronto: James Lorimer, 2005.

Government Documents

Naturalization file for Guey Dang Wong, Citizenship and Immigration Canada, including:

Confidential Report of the Royal Canadian Mounted Police, S/Cst E.H. Desaulniers, July 28, 1949.

Petition for Citizenship, Certificate of the Clerk of the Court, August 8, 1950.

Letter to New Citizens, Her Excellency the Right Honourable Michaëlle Jean, Governor General of Canada, Office of The Governor General of Canada, 2007.

Statement by Judge J. Brown, Citizenship Judge, Citizenship and Immigration Canada, 2007.

Other Sources

Annuaires Lovell de Montréal/Montreal Directory—1954. At Bibliotèque et Archives nationals. http://bibnum2.bnquebec.ca/bna/lovell/index.html.

Art Gallery of Greater Victoria, *Rice is Life* exhibit, organized by the Vancouver Museum in partnership with the Canadian Society for Asian Arts, September 19–November 23, 2008.

Cho, Karen, director. *In the Shadow of Gold Mountain.* Produced by Tamara Lynch, National Film Board of Canada, Montreal, September 2004.

Hong, Len Jung. Interviewed by Theresa Low, Vancouver, 1980. Audio Cassette T3720-0001, Royal British Columbia Museum Archives, Victoria.

Interviews and Personal Correspondence

Guan, Binghui. Eulogy for Grandma. Letter to author, December 16, 2002.

Wing, James. Interview with author, May 26, 2004, in Montreal, PQ.

Wong, Choi Yee. Interview with author, May 27, 2004, in Montreal, PQ.

Wong, King Fong. Interview with author, April 16, 2004, in Vancouver, BC.

Wong, Lai Quen. Interviews with author, various dates 2004–2009, in Victoria, BC.